THE
CHURCH
IN THE
AFRICAN
CITY

THE CHURCH IN THE AFRICAN CITY

◆

AYLWARD SHORTER

ORBIS BOOKS

Maryknoll, New York 10545

Published in the United States of America by **Orbis Books**
Maryknoll, NY 10545

Published in Great Britain by Geoffrey Chapman, an imprint of Cassell Publishers
Limited

First published 1991

Library of Congress Cataloging-in-Publication Data
Shorter, Aylward
  The Church in the African city / Aylward Shorter.
    p.   cm
  Includes bibliographical references and index.
  ISBN 0-88344-746-0
  1. Catholic Church—Africa, Sub-Saharan. 2. Pastoral theology—
Catholic Church. 3. City churches—Africa, Sub-Saharan.
4. Africa, Sub-Saharan—Church history. 5. Africa, Sub-Saharan—
Social conditions—1960– I. Title.
  BX1680.3.S56 1991
  282'.67'091732—dc20   90–47577
                                                     CIP

The Catholic Foreign Mission Society of America (Maryknoll) recruits and trains
people for overseas missionary service. Through Orbis Books Maryknoll aims to
foster the international dialogue that is essential to mission. The books published,
however, reflect the opinions of their authors and are not meant to represent the
official position of the Society.

Phototypeset by Input Typesetting Ltd., London SW19 8DR
Printed and bound in Great Britain by
Biddles Ltd, Guildford and King's Lynn

Contents

For
James Kariuki Mwangi

Introduction

Every day over 500 people are added to the population of Nairobi City, the capital of Kenya in East Africa, and most of these are new arrivals from the rural areas.[1] This statistic is an indication of the scale and rapidity of urban growth in Africa today. Africa is the least urbanized of the continents, but it is the one undergoing the most rapid urbanization. By the end of the first quarter of the next century more than half of Africa's population will be town dwelling. During the next thirty or so years we shall continue to witness the extraordinary sight of Africa's town populations doubling and redoubling in each decade, and the townships multiplying in almost every part of the continent. Urbanization is an instrument of modernization, with its concomitants of materialism and secularism. Towns and cities are centres for generating wealth, but African socio-economic realities ensure that the wealth created by urbanization is far from evenly distributed. On the contrary, there are unmistakable signs of impoverishment and disorientation caused by urbanization, and particularly by the gigantic influx of urban migrants. There are also signs that the growth and multiplication of towns is hindering valid development in the countryside.

From all of this it is clear that urbanization is the most important social reality in Africa today, and that Christian evangelization must take full account of it. The Church has turned its attention to the African town none too soon. Its own historical and theological inclinations have led it to favour the rural areas, where success has been so widely achieved. Yet the whole Christian enterprise in Africa is threatened by urbanization, and a half-hearted approach to the town will not save it. Urbanization must be taken seriously by the Church

1

and given a priority that is absolute. Personnel have to be deployed in the towns and urban Church structures created, if the Gospel is to continue to make an impact in Africa.

In contrast to the mainline Christian Churches, Islam and the various indigenous religious movements are more at home in the African town. Indeed, Islam has its own historic urban tradition on the East African coast and in West Africa, on the southern fringes of the Sahara. Indigenous religious movements easily operate as adaptive urban mechanisms for poverty-stricken migrants from the rural areas. Mainline Christianity, on the other hand, in spite of its urban origins, has had a longstanding problem of evangelizing the town in Europe and North America, quite apart from its reluctance to identify with the town in Africa. The purpose of this book is to examine the challenge that urbanization in Africa poses for the Church at the end of the twentieth century, and to suggest some strategies for future pastoral action.

My interest in the urban social realities of Africa began during my eight-year stay in Kampala City, Uganda (1968–75). There were already a number of published African urban studies, and Makerere University, where I was a part-time lecturer, had initiated several of them. Urbanization, accordingly, featured in the anthropology course that I gave as a residential lecturer at the AMECEA Pastoral Institute, then at Gaba.[2] As the AMECEA co-ordinator of the Churches' Research on Marriage in Africa 1971–76, I directed research projects in Kampala, Nairobi, Blantyre, Tabora and Soweto. In 1976 I took part in the AMECEA–AACC Urban Consultation in Nairobi.[3] For five months in 1977 I lived in Dar es Salaam City, after which I spent three years at Kipalapala Senior Seminary on the outskirts of Tabora town.

In 1981 I was asked by the Tanzania–Kenya Region of the Missionaries of Africa (White Fathers) to conduct research into the urban ministry of the society in the region. The society was involved in twenty urban parishes or projects at that time in the two countries. All the missionaries involved were circularized by the regional superior and myself, and I received from them detailed descriptions of the work being done, as well as reading lists and names of useful contacts. After spending several months doing background reading in British libraries, I returned to East Africa in September 1982, and spent the next three months visiting all the projects in Tanzania.

Travelling by road, rail and air, I spent—on average—a week in each place, covering most of Tanzania, its major towns and some of its new rural townships. I already had a long acquaintance with the country, and this enabled me to immerse myself in each working

2

situation, and even to take part in some of the tasks of urban ministry during my stay. I was received everywhere with great warmth and kindness. I spoke to three Tanzanian Catholic bishops about the research, and interviewed all the missionaries concerned, together with a number of diocesan clergy, catechists and lay people. In some cases, I visited out-stations and attended deanery meetings.

In December 1982 I flew to Nairobi, capital of Kenya, where I joined the staff of St Teresa's Catholic Parish, Eastleigh. This is numerically the largest of Nairobi's parishes and contains the notorious squatter settlement, Mathare Valley. I lived and worked in Eastleigh until August 1984, when I moved to the Catholic Higher Institute at Langata. For the next four years, until my return to Britain in 1988, I spent nearly every weekend at Eastleigh, being closely involved in parish activities. While there, I acted as chaplain to a youth group in the squatter area, and also, at the parish priest's request, ran a vocation club for boys. I studied the urban commitments of the Missionaries of Africa in Nairobi and discussed problems of urban ministry with the Cardinal Archbishop of Nairobi and numerous members of clergy and laity. I published a report on my research for the society at the end of April 1983.[4]

In 1989 and 1990 I took part in the Catholic Theological Union of Chicago's African Studies Programme in Nairobi, giving a course of lectures on Church and Urbanization in Africa, and taking up contact again with Eastleigh Parish. This enabled me to do further reading and to reflect more deeply on my own urban researches and experiences in Africa.

Over a period of twenty-five years I have travelled fairly extensively throughout the African continent to take part in conferences and lecture courses. These travels have taken me to numerous towns and cities: Johannesburg, Pretoria, Cape Town, Harare, Bulawayo, Maseru, Lusaka, Chipata, Blantyre, Lagos, Ibadan, Jos, Zaria, Kaduna, Accra, Kumasi, Yaoundé and Abidjan, as well as to many smaller urban centres. Before becoming a missionary, I paid a short visit to Cairo in 1951, and lived for two weeks in Nairobi during a four-month stay in colonial Kenya.[5] These travels and visits have given me impressions of numerous African towns and cities, in their development over the past forty years. It is an experience that has been both spatially and chronologically extensive.

This book is the fruit of all these experiences and researches. However, it understandably owes more to the project I carried out in Tanzania and Kenya in 1982–83, and to my lengthy acquaintance with the three countries of East Africa up to 1988. The result is a book that focuses on eastern Africa, while at the same time drawing parallels with towns and cities in other parts of the continent. It also draws upon several published works that deal with urbanization throughout Africa, and that compare the findings of original research in almost every region. Therefore, this is a book that deals with urban trends found in the whole of Africa, illuminated by the author's more intensive East African experience.

This book is primarily written from a Roman Catholic point of view, but it tries to draw upon the experience, contributions and researches of other Christian Churches. An entire chapter is devoted to the question of ecumenism, which assumes special importance and relevance in the African town. For eight years I belonged to an ecumenical study group in Kampala, and for five years I co-ordinated an ecumenical research project, the Churches' Research on Marriage in Africa. Sixteen Christian Churches participated in this research programme in eight African countries. In 1976 I launched the AMECEA Research Project on Ecumenical Attitudes and Initiatives in Eastern Africa, a project completed by the Reverend John Mutiso Mbinda in 1982. This book is a beneficiary of this background experience.

The first four chapters of *The Church in the African City* deal with the socio-economic realities of urbanization in Africa: the migratory basis of urban growth, the history of African towns and their socio-economic forms of life, the urban periphery, and the problem of squatter settlements. The rest of the book examines the Church's involvement with the African town: the history of this involvement, the Church's urban mission, the development of urban ecclesial structures, basic communities, the pastoral care of urban youth, and the various achievements in the field of ecumenical joint action. The final chapter sums up the main challenges that urbanization poses to Christianity in Africa, and outlines possible solutions.

I am indebted to many priests, missionaries and lay people for the material in this book, and also to students and colleagues in the various third-level institutions where I have studied and taught. I wish to express particular gratitude to the clergy, religious and laity of St Teresa's Catholic Parish, Eastleigh, Nairobi, to which I was attached for six happy and valuable years. My hope is that this book will help open Christian minds still further to the problems and possibilities of the city in Africa.

MISSIONARY INSTITUTE LONDON   AYLWARD SHORTER
                                               JULY 1990

References

1 This statistic is given by Downes *et al.* 1989, pp. 13 and 41, who suggest that births account for half the number, and migrants for the other half. The percentage of people born in the city is undoubtedly growing, but it probably does not yet equal the daily number of new migrants.

2 AMECEA is the acronym for the Association of Member Episcopal Conferences in Eastern Africa, which now comprises the episcopal conferences of Kenya, Uganda, Malawi, Tanzania, Zambia, Ethiopia and Sudan.

3 AACC stands for All-Africa Conference of Churches.

4 Shorter 1983.

5 I was a National Service officer in the King's African Rifles at the time.

1

Town and country in Africa

The Otieno burial saga

A week before Christmas 1986 a prominent Nairobi lawyer died in a car that was taking him to hospital. Nearly five months later, in April 1987, his body was still lying at the City Mortuary while a complicated legal wrangle was taking place between blood relatives and in-laws over the right to burial. The case was something of a *cause célèbre* and much has already been written about it. This is because the lawsuit touched on a number of crucial questions affecting modern Africa, not least that of urbanization. The lawyer was a member of the Luo tribe in western Kenya, a Mr Silvanus Otieno. He had, however, married Virginia Wambui, a distinguished member of the host tribe of Nairobi, the Kikuyu, and had spent the latter part of his life in the city, returning very rarely to his ancestral home in the Siaya District of Luo-land. Instead of building there, he had invested in property at Upper Matasia on the outskirts of Nairobi, and it was on this land that his widow announced her intention of burying her late husband.

Unfortunately, and perhaps uncharacteristically for a lawyer, Otieno had died intestate and, on the very day that Wambui made her funeral announcement, members of the deceased's paternal family, the Umira Kager clan, made a conflicting announcement about funeral arrangements. According to them, it would take place at Nyalgunga, a remote village in Siaya District. Wambui lost no time in obtaining a court order from a Nairobi judge forbidding the clan from taking the body. This was immediately contested by them, and in January 1987 three appeal judges issued an injunction in favour of the clan,

6

restraining Otieno's widow from carrying out the burial in any place other than Nyalgunga. Three days later Wambui filed another injunction restraining the clan, pending a full trial before Mr Justice Bosire.

The trial lasted seventeen days and testified to the extreme importance that Africans attach to everything connected with death and funerals. Ancient customs and 'superstitions' were described by witnesses for the benefit of the court and were fully reported in the press. It was alleged that a Luo tribesman could build a house in Nairobi, but never a 'home'; that no genuine Luo was ever buried outside Luo-land; that if custom was flouted, the spirit of the deceased would 'haunt' the living; and that women had no authority in any of the matters under discussion. The long line of witnesses included a herbalist, a bishop, a professor of philosophy, and even a grave-digger. At length the trial judge found for the Umira Kager clan. Nothing daunted, Wambui filed a notice of appeal on no fewer than sixteen grounds and obtained another stay of execution. The appeal hearing opened on 6 April and lasted another eleven days. On 17 April the judges ruled once more in favour of the clan and Otieno was at last buried in his rural homeland in the absence of his widow and children.

The vicissitudes of the case were followed avidly by everyone. They were the subject of conversation in every hotel, bar or kiosk. Crowds outside the law courts cheered the successive verdicts like goals in a football match. Everyone argued the issues involved: customary law versus statutory law, Christianity versus traditional beliefs, Luo versus Kikuyu, women's rights versus male chauvinism, and urban versus rural styles of living. At the heart of the dispute lay the following questions: Why should a modern, educated urban dweller who liked Shakespeare, classical music and bottled beer be subject to the customs and beliefs of a rural village? Why should he not escape the structures and strictures of tribal tradition? The answer lies in the nature of African urbanization, which consists of a close bond between urban and rural areas, a bond that not even the elite urban minority can evade.

Urbanization and urban growth: the facts

Urbanization is a form of social consciousness.[1] Kenneth Little defines it as follows: 'By urbanization is meant the process whereby people acquire material and non-material elements of culture, behaviour patterns and ideas that originate in, or are distinctive of, the city'.[2] Urban growth, on the other hand, is the physical aspect of urbanization. The term refers to the numbers of people actually living in

7

urban areas, the increase of urban populations and the multiplication of towns. In Africa today, although physically the level of urban dwelling is low in comparison with other continents, the rate of urban growth is extraordinarily high. This situation brings about a continuous interaction between town and country, and it also means that African country dwellers are being socially urbanized to an ever-increasing degree.

By the end of the twentieth century half the world's population will be urban dwelling.[3] Africa's urban level today is under 30 per cent, but by the end of the century it will probably have reached 40 per cent. The population growth rates of Africa are among the world's highest, but its urban growth rates are generally twice as high. In 1970 Africa had only seven cities of more than 1 million people. If present trends continue, by the end of the century it will have 95 such cities, five of them with more than 5 million inhabitants. In 1970, in addition to the big cities just mentioned, there were 137 towns of 100,000 or more. If present trends continue, by the end of the century there will be 692. This combination of low urban levels with high urban growth rates implies a staggering growth of existing towns — towns doubling, trebling, even quadrupling, their size in every decade. It also implies the mushrooming of towns, the spread of an urban network throughout the countryside — villages and trading centres turning into towns before our eyes.

In Chapter 4 we shall deal with some of the morbid factors of African urbanization. These include the incidence of sexually transmitted diseases, which nowadays include HIV infection and AIDS. There is little doubt that the spread of AIDS in Africa is linked, as elsewhere, to sexual promiscuity, both heterosexual and — especially in the case of North Africa — homosexual, and that prostitutes (who are numerous in the cities) are both vulnerable to infection and instrumental in spreading it. Although reliable statistics are difficult to obtain because research is both complex and politically sensitive, the thesis that urbanization and urban growth create an increased potential for AIDS is plausible.[4] It is not yet possible to say precisely how the increased mortality caused by the disease and the measures taken to combat infection are likely to affect rates of urban growth in Africa. Whatever happens to the size of national populations, patterns of urban in-migration are less likely to be affected. These may not only help to spread AIDS, but may also include the movement from rural areas of HIV-infected and AIDS sufferers to urban-based clinics and hospitals for treatment. Until now, the greatest incidence of the disease has been in certain rural areas positioned along international

8

lines of communication or associated with armed conflict, violence and rapine. There is as yet no evidence that the threat of AIDS in the towns has caused a falling-off in the influx of migrants, although it may ultimately affect the natural increase of urban populations.

Urban poverty and urban primacy

African countries are poor and high urban growth rates mean that there is a high concentration of poverty in the towns. Unlike the urban poor of Latin American cities who are a distinct and visible minority, the vast majority, perhaps 70 per cent, of African urban dwellers are poor.[5] Nevertheless, towns and cities exist in order to generate and concentrate wealth.[6] This is also true of Africa where, although the affluent elite are fighting a losing battle to maintain urban standards and services, they are nevertheless becoming richer at the expense of the urban-dwelling majority. The town is the means by which Africa is inserted as an unequal partner into the world economy. As such, it reflects this inequality at its own level.

Linked with the growing gap between rich and poor is the phenomenon of urban primacy. The so-called primate city is a historical legacy from colonialism, a single power base in a politically fragmented country from which a tiny ruling class dominated a vast territory. In countries that invited European settlement the primate city was a white enclave, with only 'servant-quarter' accommodation or low-income housing for blacks. The primate city seems to have an unlimited capacity for self-aggrandizement. After political independence it became, together with the system of government it represented, a tool of indigenous totalitarianism, and consequently the principal target for the *coup d'état*. Its social services were easier to maintain and to expand. It attracted industries that produced commodities for urban consumers. Yet, while it was materially endowed out of all proportion to the rest of the country, the primate city was unable to cope with rapid urban growth and it spawned enormous shanty-towns and squatter areas where the majority of its citizens live.

The market character of the town

Whatever one thinks of them, towns are instruments of social change and have a tendency to attract people to them. Karen Blixen, from her farm at the foot of the Ngong Hills, felt the attraction of the infant Nairobi in the 1920s, a city of around 5,000 people at that time: 'It is impossible that a town will not play a part in your life. It

9

does not matter whether you have more good or bad things to say of it, it draws your mind to it, by a mental law of gravitation.'[7]

Towns are typically markets, markets of commodities, labour markets, financial markets. They are also markets of ideas. Towns are doorways opening on to a world process of modernization, and that is one reason why towns in Africa and the developing world have a certain 'sameness' about them. They are built in the same anonymous modern styles, from the same materials, for the same purposes. Towns are centres of communication, media, information technology, tele-communications, through which new concepts and ideologies are transmitted. They are also termini or transit-stops in the transport network and import/export channels. Many of Africa's big cities are coastal and owe their sites to the historic proximity of a port. Airports, railway stations, bus stations, road haulage services, garages, mechanical workshops and fuel depots are all situated in towns.

Towns are characteristically centres of higher and/or specialized education. Whatever one means by the phrase 'human civilization'—and it usually refers to a degree of technological sophistication—it is associated with the rise of towns and the urban social consciousness. In Africa today it is probably true to say that education is the same as urbanization. The educational system urbanizes the young, gives them an urban consciousness, equips them for urban salaried employment. Consequently, centres of tertiary education, and many centres of secondary education, are located in towns. Such centres need resources that only the town can provide: libraries, laboratories, museums, cultural centres and sports facilities.

All departments of social and economic life have urban head-quarters: medical, legislative, legal, economic, financial, industrial, religious. This is because towns are power centres and the nation is organized in all aspects of its life from an urban-dwelling ruling class. Those who plan and regulate national life are town dwellers, and, in point of fact, new towns often come into existence because of the need for an administrative centre. Towns are concentrations of wealth. Banking and other financial activities take place in town. Government and public-service employees, such as teachers and social workers, are summoned to town to receive salaries, in-service training, appointments and transfers. In general terms, the town is a market for labour. It offers job opportunities in both urban and rural areas, and is a venue for interviews, training and the selection of personnel.

Finally, towns are markets in the literal sense—that is to say, centres of distribution for commodities, for local produce and local manufactures, as well as for imported goods. Regional trading centres,

10

storage depots, wholesale markets and auction rooms are located there. Moreover, towns provide a field for investment, both foreign and local. Income-generating projects of all kinds flourish in urban areas. Because of the extreme mobility of the population, one of the most lucrative forms of local investment in Africa is the building of 'guest-houses' or buildings with rooms for overnight lodging or longer-term renting.

Migration as the basis of African urban growth

When the rate of urban growth is twice that of the growth of the national population, it is probable that it is the result more of urban in-migration than of the natural increase of the town population. Around a quarter of the population of African towns was born locally, and these are mostly very small children. Nearly all urban-dwelling adults were born in the rural areas. Moreover, pregnant women still prefer to have their children in the rural homeland where this is possible. An apparent natural increase in the urban population may also be partly because of the re-drawing of city boundaries so as to include peri-urban areas. The traveller in Africa is often surprised to see a sign that reads 'The City of Lagos welcomes careful drivers' or 'Welcome to Nairobi—Green City in the Sun' far from the nearest built-up area, with the city in question nowhere in sight.

Urban in-migration is ultimately caused by national population growth and population mobility at the national level. There is a fair amount of rural-to-rural migration, as well as rural-to-urban. Town populations are also far from stable. Besides in-migration, there is also out-migration, both urban-to-rural and urban-to-urban (other towns). All in all, net in-migration continues to grow rapidly and massively, although natural increase is beginning to take a larger share in the total growth of urban populations.[8]

Urban in-migration can be studied both spatially and temporally. That is to say, it can be analysed in the light of the geographical origins of the migrants and the duration of their stay in town. Spatial patterns reveal that most migrants originate in the rural area adjacent to the town itself, the homeland of the so-called 'host tribe'.[9] Most of the others originate in distant regions which suffer from overcrowding, and consequently from shortages of food and essential commodities. The fact that migration may be either short-distance or long-distance also affects the stability of urban populations in Africa. The short-distance migrant may find it easier to identify with the town in the long term. Temporal patterns reveal that the majority of migrants

11

are short-stay urban dwellers. In spite of this, there is a growing core of committed urban dwellers in African towns—people like Silvanus Otieno, who have made the town their permanent base. Paradoxically, it is probable that both long-stay and short-stay in-migration are increasing at the same time.[10] Generally, however, rural-to-urban migration differs from the rural-to-rural variety, in that the latter envisages a more or less permanent stay in a new village settlement, while the urban migrant frequently envisages only a short stay in town.

Another difference is that rural-to-rural migration usually involves whole families. This is only true of long-term urban in-migration. Short-term urban in-migration is characterized by an unbalanced sex ratio and by a preponderance of young migrants. Although opportunities for women in Africa are improving and the proportion of female short-term migrants is increasing, there is an absolute increase of males over females, and nearly half the migrants are between the ages of fourteen and nineteen. Most of these young people are looking for education or employment. These patterns contribute to the unbalanced sex and age structures found in African towns. Often there is an excess of males and a preponderance of young adults. The typical age structure of an African town is one in which around 85 per cent are under the age of thirty, with young adults between the ages of twenty and twenty-nine accounting for 30 per cent. Adults in their thirties and forties constitute 10 per cent, while the over-fifties are a mere 5 per cent.

An unbalanced urban age and sex structure is the cause of many problems connected with sexual and family morality. However, it is by no means the only unfortunate result of accelerated urban growth in Africa. The most obvious consequence is the desperate need for housing and social services. The huge squatter settlements in African cities bear witness to the failure to cater for these. The influx of cheap, unskilled labour affects the scale of urban production and the balance between large-scale and small-scale activities. Whether or not there is an increase in production is uncertain, but there is no doubt at all about increased consumption, the rise in the number of unemployed and under-employed. The search for casual employment is the chief occupation of the young migrant to an African town.

Positive and negative images of the town

It is not surprising, then, that negative images of the town are more persistent than positive ones. José Comblin has examined most of the pejorative labels attached by pessimistic urban sociologists to varieties of town.[11] Towns are seen as oppressive, parasitical and proletarianizing, even as 'theatres of death', an epithet that is not undeserved when one considers that a capital city is often the prime military target in a civil war or *coup d'état*. Kampala City, for example, the Ugandan capital, has been captured and recaptured in the successive sieges of recent years. In a phrase attributed to Mao Tse Tung, towns and cities in the developing world have been described as the 'rubbish heaps of bourgeois civilization'. When one contemplates all the morbid factors of African urban life one is tempted to agree—insanitary living conditions, rush-hour traffic jams, over-burdened communications networks, parking problems, extortionate rents, violent crime, juvenile delinquency, prostitution, sexually transmitted disease, drug-trafficking and so forth. Frequently, a nightmare picture is presented of a 'town without a master', a cancerous growth that cannot be halted or brought under control.

While there is truth in the nightmare, it must be admitted that towns would not continue to grow and to attract people if they did not offer the migrant some advantage. It is probably true to say that urban in-migration is materially beneficial to the migrant. Presumably, there is a reasonable chance that the migrant will improve his or her income. However, the total influx is too great for an even distribution of wealth among urban employees, or between town and country. The enormous flow of migrants means that job-seekers outnumber job opportunities. Labour remains cheap and rents high. Urban in-migration benefits the rich urban employer and landlord far more than it benefits the migrant. Moreover, although migrants send remittances back to the rural areas, most of the wealth created by migration remains concentrated in the town and is not spread evenly throughout the country as a whole. Whereas towns and cities in capitalist Europe or North America are able to generate income for the rest of the country, the urban phenomenon in Africa encourages internal exploitation.[12]

Nevertheless, town life offers the migrant a promise of liberty and multiplicity of choice in addition to personal enrichment. The town is a remarkable accumulation of projects which are the product of human collaboration. Lewis Mumford, who is largely optimistic about urbanization, has described the birth of the town as a 'mutation' for humanity. It certainly does represent a leap forward in the history of human collaborative enterprise. Even in Africa, the core of long-term urban residents—such as Silvanus Otieno in Nairobi—continues to grow. It would be altogether an exaggeration to say that the African town is a vehicle for unalloyed beneficial change. However, it would

13

also be unrealistic to ignore its potential for positive human development.

Rural–urban reinforcement in Africa

Western observers often assume that there is a conflict between urban and rural interests in Africa. While it is true that income generation favours the town-based elite, this does not preclude a large measure of urban–rural reinforcement or mutual support. The assumption that urban growth in Africa must follow historic Western patterns is patently false. If there is one characteristic that stands out as differentiating African towns from those in other continents, it is that there are close socio-economic ties between urban and rural areas in Africa. In Chapter 3 we shall see how the phenomenon of peri-urbanization favours the spread of an urban consciousness in the countryside. Here we shall examine the rural postulates of African urban growth. The basic truth is that African town dwellers never really sever their ties with the rural homeland. As we saw at the beginning of this chapter, Wambui ultimately lost her case against her deceased husband's rural family. To understand the urban migrant in Africa one must know his or her rural background. This is no mere cultural romanticism, no simple idealization of the village world. Romanticism has not been lacking, either among Western observers and environmentalists or among African political ideologues. Not many years ago, villagization was so important a dogma in Tanzania that the city of Dar es Salaam was divided into nine administrative 'villages'. It was not long before this absurd division was found unworkable and the municipal authority restored. The unromantic truth is that urban growth is a necessary, if not crucial, component of agricultural development. The agricultural sector of the national economy is almost entirely governed by an urban-based elite and by capital, policy and technology that originate in, or are channelled through, the towns. This fact alone makes the town attractive to the migrant from the rural areas. Farming in Africa is not the preserve of a small, professional, landed class. The vast majority of the national population possesses land, is engaged in peasant farming and grows its own staple food as well as the increasingly frequent cash crop.

African town dwellers are basically rural-to-urban migrants. Many are short-term migrants who come to town for education, for medical treatment, or to find casual employment through which to improve the family income. The trip to town may even be a kind of 'initiation rite' for modern youth who cannot hold up their heads at

14

home in the village without first seeing the big city. Even when the migrant becomes a long-term urban resident, he or she pays frequent visits to the rural homeland. The migrant always retains contact with this base and consorts with other migrants from the same region. The motives that draw the migrant to the city are primarily economic; those that draw him back to the rural homeland are primarily social and cultural. Of this trend the Otieno burial saga is a paradigm. The transience of the urban population is partly related to job mobility. The migrant is an opportunist in a situation of intense job competition. Often the job is a casual one anyway, or the worker may lose his job or be laid off rather easily. Again, migrants move from job to job, and from town to town, in order to improve their income. In this situation of transience and uncertainty the focus of interest remains the rural homeland.

Urban migrants make frequent visits to the rural homeland, especially if it is adjacent to the town itself. Obviously, long-distance migrants are obliged to make less frequent journeys, though their sojourn in the rural area is likely to be of longer duration. A survey taken in Nairobi City in 1986 revealed that a majority of the population paid at least five visits a year to the rural areas.[13] People participate in rural social and family events. They tend to return to the homeland in order to marry, give birth or retire. Usually, they maintain a rural family home as well as an urban residence. There was no doubt in the minds of witnesses in the Otieno lawsuits that a Luo tribesman's home could never be his town residence.

It was also said that members of the Luo tribe were never buried outside their homeland. While this may not be strictly true, Wambui's lawyers had trouble finding exceptions. Urban cemeteries in Africa are mostly used by non-Africans. Bereaved relatives go to great effort and expense to send the corpse home for burial. There are virtually no undertakers in African towns, but municipal mortuaries play an important role in housing the remains of the deceased while travel and funeral arrangements are being made and/or litigation is taking place. In some cases a Requiem Mass, memorial service or leave-taking takes place in town before the body is exported for burial. Public service vehicles are so frequently requisitioned for funeral transport that this aspect of their service may be advertised. There is at least one such vehicle in Nairobi with the name 'Coffin Carrier' emblazoned on it.

It is argued by urban sociologists that the migrant's stability in town depends on an expectation of future interaction and exchange with others over a long period of time. Without such an expectation,

15

the town dweller does not feel secure and may terminate urban residence. The interaction and exchange envisaged seldom take place in town alone, unless it coincides with a sufficient urban family income and the migration to town of a viable proportion of the extended family. Much more commonly, the urban migrant envisages a continued interaction and exchange with relatives and acquaintances in the rural homeland. Two well-known exponents of African urban anthropology have demonstrated that the degree to which an African urban resident is stabilized depends on the extent to which he or she is able to maintain participation in rural life without impossibly long absences from town.[14] If the tension between urban and rural participation becomes too great, then out-migration to the rural area takes place. The ultimate focus of the urban migrant remains rural.

The rural family community is also usually the urban migrant's last insurance when he or she encounters economic failure in town. However, people who experience such failure may be tempted to embark on a life of crime rather than return empty-handed to the home village. The violent criminal is typically the young man who enjoys an urban life-style beyond his legitimate means. Even when the law catches up with him, he finds concealment easier in the 'anonymous' town than in the home village where he is known. This raises the more general question of what are called the 'push–pull' causes of urban in-migration.

Push–pull factors in migration

As we have seen, one of the factors that push the migrant away from the home village is rural overcrowding. In many African countries, however, there is plenty of land of poor quality to be had. The farmer has simply to clear the bush to make good his title to a farm. It is the more fertile, highland or lakeside areas that are densely populated where the frontier of landlessness is encroaching on the community. A good example is provided by the highland areas of Kisii in western Kenya or of the Kikuyu in Central Province. The Chagga of Kilimanjaro and the Nyakyusa of the Southern Highlands of Tanzania, the Ganda and the Kiga of Uganda afford other examples. A journey through the Kisii or Kiga Highlands reveals how every inch of fertile land, even the topmost slopes of high hills, is under terrace cultivation. In these places violent family quarrels over the division of inherited farms are commonplace, and there is considerable rural out-migration.

Many urban migrants, however, come from thinly populated rural areas where the soil is of poor quality, and from the so-called 'mar-

16

ginal' or semi-arid areas where scratching a living from the soil is the only prospect for the peasant farmer. The marginal areas are also the homelands of cattle-herding nomads who may not be above short-term urban migration in order to replenish their livestock in a lean year. During a widespread drought a few years ago, the cattle-herding Maasai of East Africa grazed their animals on the outskirts of highland townships in Kenya and Tanzania, and many took up temporary employment as nightwatchmen or as members of cultural displays for tourists in the towns. The push factor in the thinly populated regions is the lack of prospects caused by deficiencies of one kind or another.

Nevertheless, it would be wrong to see the urban migrant as simply a refugee from rural distress. The pull factors are usually stronger than the push factors. The town offers better prospects, more opportunities for improving the family income. As O'Connor puts it, the basic cause of migration is the 'perceived differential' between one area and another.[15] People move in order to secure higher rewards for their labour. While it is true that rural out-migration may be essential in certain overcrowded rural areas, most migrants have a choice, and they exercise that choice in favour of a move to town.

People seek employment in town. They also seek education and the benefit of social services, particularly medical treatment and health care. As we have seen, educational and medical services are centred, for various reasons, on the town. In developing countries, networks of distribution frequently break down, as a result of transport failures or, in some cases, corruption. This creates shortages of commodities in the rural areas and encourages people to migrate to the towns that are the sources of these commodities. We have seen that the town is a field for local investment. This usually takes the form of urban leisure facilities such as restaurants, bars, discos, lodging-houses and rooms for renting. Provision of such facilities is itself a consequence of urban growth.

For many young men and women, the desire for freedom from social constraints in close-knit rural communities is the primary motive for migration. Curiosity about, or attraction to, urban values, as well as enhanced social status, can also be important. Some migrants move in order to join families in town. This is especially true of wives and children. In many cases, children are sent to school in town by rural parents, because it is believed—probably rightly—that urban educational standards are higher and job prospects better at the town school. It is true to say that in Africa today towns are no longer alien places for most people. Africans are increasingly at home with town

17

life. In some instances they even feel physically more secure in the town than in the countryside.

In spite of all this, towns are still often colonial in origin and are seen by migrants as essentially work-places. African townspeople are still attached to their homeland in the rural area. When employment ceases they can return there. The old can go back there to a position of influence and esteem. The farm in the homeland, especially if it is adjacent to the town, is often a subsidiary source of food for town dwellers. Since women are responsible for food production, they often remain in the rural areas, looking after the farm and visiting their husbands in town during the slack season. One of the biggest obstacles to family migration, as opposed to the migration of individual family members, is the cost of urban housing and urban living. As a result, families are divided and bachelor households abound in town. A large proportion of female migrants have no husband to join and set up house on their own, or with their children. There is no doubt, as we shall see in Chapter 9, that urban in-migration has a devastating effect on family life and morality.

Ronald Frankenberg coined the term 'spiralism'.[16] It refers to people who are continually striving to better their economic and social position. In Africa it probably applies more particularly to the elite, who are the most mobile class. They tend to move from town to town and from post to post, moving up the table of salary scales. A member of the elite spends all his life in town, and yet he seems to belong to no town in particular. His focus of interest may remain firmly rural, centred in fact upon a retirement home or holiday villa in the rural homeland. His wealth enables him to travel there more often and to invest in agricultural and other projects there. If he is a politician, this rural interest and rural patronage may be an important condition for building himself a power-base. Spiralism affects the lower-income brackets as well. Individuals who are successful adopt better standards of housing and eventually move to middle-income neighbourhoods within the city. Yet massive and increasing in-migration ensures that the majority of Africa's town dwellers remain poor.

The rural–urban continuum

There is no doubt that the fates of both town and countryside are bound up together in Africa, and that there is a measure of urban–rural reinforcement. Towns are centres for the generation and redistribution—admittedly, uneven—of wealth in countries that are massively agricultural. The question of how this rural–urban continuum affects

18

the socio-economic development of the countryside will be considered in greater detail in Chapter 3, with the phenomenon of peri-urbanization. There is a sense in which whole African countries are becoming 'peri-urbanized'. In this first chapter we have looked at the basic causes of urban growth and urbanization in Africa. These are all bound up with urban in-migration. A first question to ask, therefore, is what consequences this phenomenon has for the countryside. Urban in-migration necessarily entails rural out-migration. What impact does this have on the welfare of rural communities?

The loss of manpower is not necessarily injurious. In areas of overcrowding, pressure is relieved on the growing rural population. Remittances are sent home by those who find employment in the town. The families of migrants are often much better off than those of non-migrants. However, just as urban in-migration tends to prolong colonial patterns of short-term labour, so the subsidizing of agriculture by urban incomes tends to be exploitive of the subsistence farmer in the long run. This is even more the case if a measure of commercialization of agriculture is one of the outcomes of migration.

The social consequences are more severe. The absence of parents affects family education adversely and undermines the authority of elders. This is offset in some instances by the return of young migrants when they inherit land. These returnees have built up capital through urban employment. Where the land is sufficiently fertile, such a return may entail no significant loss of income. It also helps to stabilize families and strengthen their bonds with the homeland. It can thus be seen that there are many interlocking factors between town and country in Africa, that there is a rural–urban continuum, and that urban growth and urbanization in Africa affect the whole of national life.

From here we shall go on, in Chapter 2, to look at the history and typology of the African town and the forms of social and cultural life that are characteristic of it. Chapters 3 and 4 deal with peri-urbanization and what has been called 'urbanization from below'. Only then can we begin to assess the role of the Church in what is probably the most significant contemporary trend in the socio-cultural life of Africa.

References

1 I prefer to follow Professor Kenneth Little's definition of urbanization, rather than those who, like Anthony O'Connor, equate it

with what I prefer to call 'urban growth'. Cf. Little 1974, pp. 4–5 and O'Connor 1983 (1986), pp. 17–18.

2 Little 1974, p. 7.

3 For the trends given here, cf. Zanotelli 1988.

4 Clarke 1988, pp. 108–12, links urbanization with the spread of AIDS in Africa. In Cosstick 1987, Nunn suggests (p. 26) that arguments for the urbanization linkage in Africa based on blood donation are unreliable.

5 O'Connor 1983, pp. 20–21, suggests that 10–15 per cent belong to the middle income range and 5 per cent to the affluent elite.

6 Cf. Gilbert and Gugler 1981 (1989), p. 11.

7 Blixen 1937 (1980), p. 22.

8 Cf. O'Connor 1983 (1986), pp. 57–98, for a full discussion of all the factors connected with urban in-migration in Africa.

9 The term 'host' was coined by David Parkin. Cf. Parkin 1969 and 1975, *passim*.

10 O'Connor 1983 (1986), p. 68.

11 Comblin 1968.

12 Cf. Gilbert and Gugler 1981 (1989), p. 11.

13 This survey was conducted by students of Daystar University College in the Mathare Valley and Kariobangi squatter areas of Nairobi's Eastlands. Cf. Downes *et al.* 1989.

14 Clyde-Mitchell 1969; Mayer 1961.

15 O'Connor 1983 (1986), p. 74.

16 Frankenberg 1966, *passim*.

2

The town in Africa—history and typology

Africa's pre-colonial towns

On 10 April 1875 the explorer Henry Morton Stanley first beheld the capital of the Ganda King, the indigenous settlement out of which the modern city of Kampala, capital of Uganda, has since developed.[1] He was astonished to find himself treading a broad road of beaten earth that led up to an imposing hill crowned with large conical buildings, in the centre of which rose 'a lofty barn-like structure' that turned out to be the royal palace. The dwellings were surrounded by tall fences of cane and there were broad avenues thronged by people in picturesque costume. Stanley was amazed by the roads, the court-yards, and the enclosures of King Mutesa's capital on Rubaga Hill, an indigenous town with a population of 5,000.

Pre-colonial Africa was thus not without its urban communities, which were usually an adjunct of well-developed monarchical states, like that of the Ganda. Under the influence of the ancient Egyptian and Meroitic culture, urban life became a feature of the so-called Sudanic civilization, as well as of the medieval states of Guinea. One example is that of the Nigerian Yoruba who have lived in towns for centuries. These towns were extensive and strongly fortified against attack. The pattern was one of rectangular compounds in which related families lived together. The townsmen, however, lived by farming the periphery of the town, and many also had temporary dwellings in the vicinity of their farms. We shall see in Chapter 3 how this peri-urbanization survives in the modern African town. Each of the Yoruba towns was ruled by a king and was in fact the capital of a kingdom which was itself a network of smaller towns whose chiefs were subject to the king at the capital. The king lived in a palace, which was effectively the largest compound of the town.

Under the influence of the Coptic Church, indigenous Christian towns developed in medieval Sudan and Ethiopia. These were also the capitals of local rulers. Addis Ababa, the best known among the surviving examples, was originally the indigenous capital city of the Ethiopian king. Muslim influence, however, was responsible for a more widespread pre-colonial urbanization. Along the southern fringes of the Sahara Desert, and down the coast of eastern Africa, towns like Djenné and Timbuktu, Mombasa and Kilwa grew up as inland or coastal emporia. Islamic culture in Africa was, and is, essentially urban.

Contrast such ancient urban traditions with the birth of a European town like Johannesburg, Nairobi or Lusaka. Nairobi, for example, came into existence in 1899 as a transport depot for the construction of the Uganda Railway. Its site was a bleak stretch of marshy landscape straddling the insignificant Nairobi river, without a tree in sight but with vast herds of wild animals grazing on the surrounding plains. It is to Sergeant Ellis of the Royal Engineers that the honour of founding Nairobi belongs. His small camp became the location of a temporary railhead while the railway builders pushed up into the highlands and the escarpment beyond. Everything about Nairobi in the early years was temporary. Indeed, there was at first a discussion about moving the town to a more salubrious site. The city took root more by default than by design.

It is hard nowadays to imagine the void that pre-existed the modern Nairobi, with its high-rise buildings, impressive sky-line and 2 million inhabitants. The creation of such cities *ex nihilo*, as it were, is a direct consequence of modernization. In other instances, ancient indigenous or Islamic towns have either been modernized or have had a modern town annexed to them. In either case, their character has been altered. Very few of the pre-colonial towns have escaped dramatic and sweeping change. Those that have avoided it or that have changed more slowly and imperceptibly may resemble Southall's type 'A' town.[2] Let us now consider the question of an urban typology for Africa.

An African urban typology

Southall's urban typology, proposed more than a quarter of a century ago, is a simple dual categorization. Type 'A' is the old, slowly growing town, well integrated with the surrounding rural areas. This type, though increasingly rare, can still be said to exist. An example might be provided by Tabora in Tanzania, the town founded by nineteenth-century Arab traders near the headquarters of the Nyamwezi chief of Unyanyembe. Such a town is receptive to rural influences, rather than itself transforming the surrounding areas. Like the traditional Yoruba towns of Nigeria, many of the inhabitants are still farmers. In the case of Tabora, many are employed in educational establishments, schools and colleges. These incapsulated communities with a transient student membership make little impact outside the town. In general, there is no cultural hiatus with the rural areas. From the point of view of occupation and focus of interest, it remains visibly circumscribed, even rustic, a 'town that is a village'.[3]

Southall's other category, type 'B', is the new town, or town that has experienced rapid and recent mushroom growth. This type clearly needs to be divided. Perhaps the two types 'A' and 'B' should even be treated as poles in a spectrum, with a variety of intermediate forms. Towns can grow rapidly in different ways. Some simply enlarge their boundaries as more and more migrants swell the population. Their influence is magnetic, but there is a greater or lesser hiatus between them and their surroundings. Other towns, while growing in size themselves, exercise a strong and extensive influence in the surrounding region, creating services, siting industries and encouraging the growth of satellite towns.

Another typology of the African town is that of Oram.[4] This is based on its social and economic functions, rather than on its rate and manner of growth. However, as soon as one looks for examples, one realizes that none of his types exists in a pure form. Basically, they are fourfold. The administrative town contains the headquarters of central or local government and its population is largely employed in the public services: civil service, police, prisons, armed forces, municipal workers, railways and so forth. Probably, many, if not most, African towns would qualify for this type.

The agricultural service town exists primarily to market agricultural produce, to organize agriculture and rural settlement, to provide farm implements, seed, fertilizer, veterinary services and technical advice or supervision. It may also be the location for the growing number of agricultural processing industries. In developing countries this type of town is home to an agricultural bureaucracy, which renders it indistinguishable from the administrative town.

The commercial town is Oram's third category. It goes without saying that all towns are more or less commercial. However, in certain cases the predominant emphasis may be commercial, whether it be import–export, wholesaling, or banking, credit and finance. The bigger cities, especially those that are ports or rail junctions, cannot fail to be involved in the movement and distribution of goods for sale.

The fourth category, the industrial town, is divided into two: manufacturing and mining. The specialized manufacturing town hardly exists in Africa, not in any degree comparable with, say, the Lancashire cotton towns in England. Most of the bigger cities have recognizable industrial or manufacturing areas, but in some cases these spill over into satellite manufacturing towns. Thika town, with its cloth mills and textile factory, in the vicinity of Nairobi City, might offer an example. Generally, however, the African industrial town is a mining town. Johannesburg, one of Africa's greatest cities, was originally a mining town, and the mining compounds with their great mountains of excavated yellow sand still surround the city. Mining towns are traditionally divided into compounds, which are self-sufficient total societies in themselves. They are a town within the town, providing their own housing and their own commercial and social services to the employees. The towns of the Zambian and Zairean Copperbelt fit this description.

Besides not being exclusive, Oram's categories are not exhaustive. One encounters towns with other social and economic functions—the educational town, for example, or even the medical town built around a district hospital. Equally excluded is the indigenous town or the religious town (usually Islamic), with its focus on a shrine or holy place. Perhaps a more satisfactory criterion for an urban typology in Africa is that of history and culture. This is the basis for O'Connor's scheme.[5]

O'Connor lists six types of African city. The indigenous city was originally a centre of pre-colonial and pre-Islamic administrative and political power. It was usually associated with divine kingship and may even have been a mobile city, moving with the king and his court. This was the case with the Rubaga, which Stanley visited in Uganda in 1875. Successive Ganda kings established their courts on successive hills in the Kampala area. Colonial rule had the effect of stabilizing these indigenous capitals.

The Islamic city was the consequence of the immigrant religion of Islam and its characteristically urban culture. It is found in the savannah and Sahel regions of West Africa and on the East African coast. As O'Connor rightly points out, African initiatives remained dominant in the development of these towns and all, except the most remote, received stronger alien influences in the colonial period.

The colonial city, as its name implies, arose out of the colonial experience. This type dates from the end of the nineteenth century, at the earliest, when long-distance colonial trade began and lines of communication (particularly railways) were set up. In some cases, indigenous or Islamic cities were converted into colonial cities, but many were 'creations *ex nihilo*'. Such towns were originally administrative and the participation of the African majority was exercised within the framework of white minority rule. At independence, all the structures of this type of city were retained, as were the economic links with Europe. The racial zones that characterized the colonial city were maintained on a basis of wealth and class. The European residential zone, in particular, is today occupied by Westernized Africans of high income.

The European city is simply a special case of the colonial city. It was colonial in the strict sense, being a centre of permanent European settlement. In this type of city the attempt was made to exclude long-term African residents. Often it was a replica of the modern town in Europe and reflected contemporary town-planning ideas. This type of town has proved most vulnerable in the long run to the dramatic influx of African migrants after political independence, and although independent governments attempted to carry on the Draconian policies of the colonial regime to deter migrants, the worst squatter areas are found in this type of town.

O'Connor's two final categories are combinations of preceding types. The dual city combines two or more; for example, indigenous–colonial and Islamic–colonial. These are maintained as separate and distinct cultural sectors, with a measure of interaction between them. At independence, the distinction between the sectors often became blurred. Examples are Khartoum in Sudan, Kano in Nigeria and, until 1966, Kampala in Uganda. The hybrid city is one in which there is a convergence of different cultural sectors. In some cases, it was formerly a dual city.

Typologies, such as these we have been considering, help us to realize how varied in origins, patterns of growth and socio-economic functions is the African town. We now take a look at the social and cultural differences between urban and rural areas.

Culture and anti-culture in the African town

It is often assumed that the African city is a cultural melting-pot, and that there is such a thing as a developing African urban culture. Closer examination of the reality suggests that stew might be a better image than melting-pot. In a stew the various ingredients retain their individual identity. First, it has to be said that urbanization is basically a social process or consciousness and that it has a marked effect on people's ways of life. Urbanization, therefore, affects culture. As a result of social change, modern Africans find themselves culturally disoriented. Although they feel the need to identify with their traditional ethnic cultures and see them as somehow normative, they also realize that they need to be redefined in the context of modernization. It is the urban experience that is the principal vehicle for change and modernization in contemporary Africa. Therefore, it is understandable that town-dwelling Africans should feel the cultural disorientation most acutely.

Town-dwelling Africans, as we saw in Chapter 1, are still in direct contact with their ethnic cultural traditions. Urbanization does not substitute a new modern culture for the old traditional one. What it does is to modify the traditional culture of town dwellers and, to a lesser extent, that of rural dwellers. The urban consciousness denotes a predilection for new concepts and forms of behaviour in which there is a greater degree of individual choice and an increase in personal autonomy and creativity. There is no doubt that all of this erodes traditional concepts and patterns of behaviour. Moreover, there is a measure of non-simultaneity in absorbing and synthesizing the new elements. Cultural disorientation is partly a result of the fact that Africans are living in two semi-incapsulated worlds at the same time. At the level of the industrial technical, or of the leisure ethic, they accept foreign ideas and norms, while at the domestic level they remain true to their traditional ideals, values and world-view. Urbanization, therefore, does not provide people with a new culture. Rather, it gives people the consciousness of an extra cultural dimension which is not easily integrated with ethnic tradition.

The ability to transform developing scientific knowledge into technology is what is called modernization and it lies at the heart of the international socio-economic system of which African towns are a part. Modernization imposes common patterns and common solutions on urban development and urban living. It is responsible for the visible similarity of modern towns, be they in Europe or in Africa. To a great extent modernization is a neutral currency that can serve any or every cultural value system.

However, it is not entirely value-free. In fact, it is heir to the development of ideas and behavioural norms of the Western world which still jealously controls it. Some of these are positive: freedom of choice, personal autonomy, women's rights, non-violence and other liberal attitudes. Others are subversive of non-Western cultures: acquisitiveness, consumerism, commercialism, individualism, materialism, secularism. Modernization inculcates the assumption that the only truths are scientific truths, and it induces an attitude towards the natural world that has been described as one of plunder not wonder.[6] In other words, it exploits—and even poisons—the environment. It places an absolute value on material possessions, on leisure, comfort, pleasure and immediate satisfaction. It encourages transience and superficiality in human relationships and it privatizes and relativizes moral and spiritual beliefs and values. Modernization is also the major Western instrument of world domination, and it is channelled via education, the communications media and the leisure industries.

The Fathers of the Second Vatican Council spoke of 'more universal forms of culture' coming into existence.[7] This view echoed the optimism of urban sociologists like Lewis Mumford who saw urban development as producing a better and more comfortable life for everyone.[8] Much of the contemporary talk about 'the global village' makes the same assumption. As soon as one examines the realities of urban life in Africa, one sees that it offers no grounds for a universal culture and still less for a solution to human poverty and the imbalance of wealth in the world. Urbanization does not automatically integrate ethnic cultures, nor can it cope with the massive poverty of rural–urban migrants.

On the contrary, a case can be made out for urbanization as a contributor to a universal anti-culture, a movement that erodes and undermines traditional cultures, by impoverishing them, diminishing human sensibilities, devaluing primary symbols and substituting material for moral and spiritual goals. By creating material slums, it begets spiritual slums, and promotes cultural ignorance and degradation. The culture it creates is one of silence and desperate survival. One of the most devastating examples the world has seen in recent years was the enforced urbanization and modernization by the Ceauşescu regime of Romania which set out to destroy the rural culture of the people.

On the other hand, in most cases African urban areas are not just places of dereliction and despair. They are also places of opportunity and innovation. Much depends on the attitude of the urban migrant. The cultural pluralism of the African town may engender a ghetto mentality or an attitude of disorientation and drift. It also provides a basis for a dialectic or exchange, a dialogue of lived experience. This does not result in the genesis of a new culture, or in the coalescence of old cultures, but it makes each ethnic culture a field

27

of encounter with others. It identifies lines of agreement, teaches new interests and encourages the growth of multiculturalism. As we shall see in Chapter 6, the urban mission of the African Church lies in this direction.

Social organization in town and country

There is no doubt that urban living has a marked effect on a person's way of life. Inhuman living conditions and the imbalance of ages and sexes lead to a disruption of family life. The fact that church marriage rates tend to be higher in urban than in rural areas may, in fact, indicate an expectation of marital instability, rather than the reverse. Church marriage may be sought as an ally against destabilizing influences, particularly family pressure from the rural areas. Since many crucial relatives are not present in town, urban dwellers are forced to operate with a truncated extended family. Family roles are telescoped. Yet there is a tendency for individuals to attract kinsfolk to town and this may gradually lead to a better representation of the family community. Over several generations perhaps half the family community will have migrated to town. For the time being, many households are all-bachelor households, and those that are not are headed by women, in the absence of a husband, father or brother.

The urban migrant makes other contacts besides kinsfolk, with workmates, classmates, fellow-villagers from the same rural homeland. These networks, as we shall see, take the place of, or supplement, family relationships. In spite of many hardships, young migrants really love town life. For them it represents a continual round of leisure pursuits, making music and dancing. There are also social events that bring people together: sport, funerals, mourning. Church services, outdoor religious gatherings and processions are popular and so are events organized by the many schools and educational establishments. Above all, the town is the stage for exciting political events, rallies, polling, demonstrations, VIP visits and so forth. Where relatively cohesive ethnic communities survive in town, traditional rituals may even be carried out. Dewey has shown how life-crisis rituals survive in town because they are often ego-centred rites of passage.[9]

An amusing example that proves this point occurred in Nairobi in May 1985. Kikuyu circumcision rituals were organized at Wakulima wholesale market in a campaign that lasted four months. Porters at the market alleged that some of their colleagues were behaving in a childish and immature manner. Apparently, they did not always display sufficient honesty and courtesy in their dealings with clients. After investigation, it was found that the culprits were not circumcised, so their fellow porters organized the required social maturity ritual, and nine candidates were taken to city clinics for the operation amid singing and jubilation. It was felt that the traditional ritual would discourage antisocial behaviour and enhance the dignity of the market porters' profession.[10]

In general, however, there are profound differences between social organization in town and country. Urban society follows the associative, rather than the cohesive, principle. In the village a new arrival finds a ready-made community which he is obliged to accept if he wishes to live there. The anonymity of the town allows the migrant to fashion an ego-centred network of patrons and clients. Physical proximity is not socially privileged, as it is in the rural neighbourhood. Urban dwellers create their own selective neighbourhoods of chosen associates. In the rural areas there is little specialization, apart from the traditional sex-division of labour. In town, on the other hand, there is a high degree of specialization. Social life in the rural areas has a locality-focus—the place of residence. In towns, it more often has a work-focus—the place of employment. In the rural areas social status is ascribed, that is to say, a resident's social position is assumed and an appropriate behaviour is expected. In the town social status is achieved, that is to say, it derives from the migrant's behaviour and work performance. In rural areas norms of behaviour are commonly imposed and accepted. This is not the case in town, where there is always some measure of alienation from traditional behavioural norms. People adopt alien norms, or invent their own.

By exception, a certain measure of social cohesion appears or reappears in town, particularly in the squatter settlements and low-income areas. This is caused by the experience of shared poverty and the relative specialization imposed by self-employment. Occasionally, it coincides with the existence of a so-called ethnic village. This is one of the adaptive mechanisms or bridges between rural and urban living that enable migrants to adapt to a new mode of life: ethnic welfare associations, funeral societies, community centres, clubs and associations of all kinds, also churches, particularly the new religious movements or Independent Churches, and mission-related Churches with a strong ethnic affiliation.

We have seen that African towns have varied economic functions. The structure of their economy may therefore be described in various ways. O'Connor's terminology is probably the most comprehensive.[11] The basic division is between the large-scale and small-scale sectors. The large-scale sector, which is divided into public and private, deals with financial, manufacturing and commercial enterprises that concern both home and overseas constituencies. The small-scale sector, which deals with small-scale businesses and forms of self-employment, is also divided between traditional activities, such as traditional crafts and the vending of traditional medicines, and modern informal enterprises, such as the retailing of vegetables or the running of food kiosks. There is often an intermediate sector, straddling both public and private, that includes such activities as food production, construction and transport. The small-scale sector communicates mainly with producers and customers in the homeland. In the city there is an interchange of goods and services between the representatives of the various economic sectors.

Urban society is highly stratified. The strata in African towns are incipient classes based on the socio-economic system. At the top of the scale are the new elite and the ruling, professional and managerial classes. Lower down the scale are the secretarial staffs, the artisans, tradesmen, manual workers, stall-holders, truckers, carriers, messengers and the semi-literate in general. The principle of spiralism described in Chapter 1 somewhat mitigates the latent hostility that exists between these strata.

Ethnicity in the African city

The African city is poly-ethnic and is a crucible for ethnic cultures. In many ways it is a 'laboratory' for national culture. Racial differences are less important than ethnic ones, except in southern Africa. In the independent countries, Africans constitute a massive majority over other races in the urban areas. In fact, Africanization has broken the link that existed in colonial times between the immigrant races and high incomes. Today, the most affluent town dwellers are likely to be the small group of African elite. Asians in East Africa combine a separate racial identity with cultural and religious traditions that set them apart. This, together with their virtual commercial monopoly, has made them unpopular. In general, minority racial groups—Europeans, Asians, Lebanese, Arabs, Chinese—form distinct communities with minimum social communication.

African tribal identity is expressed through loyalty to particular traditions or institutions, such as initiation rites, wedding ceremonies and funeral customs. However, vernacular languages constitute the fundamental barrier to social integration in town. Some authors argue that urbanization entails detribalization. Others, on the contrary, maintain that it results in tribal reinforcement. In general, this is a barren

30

discussion. The fact is that urban living transforms ethnic identities and gives them new scope and new areas of application, especially in the networks that we consider in the next section of this chapter. Ethnic pluralism can have contradictory effects. In one instance it dilutes traditional culture. In another case it makes the individual more ethnically conscious, especially if he or she belongs to a minority. It is sometimes said that a new generation of detribalized children is coming into existence in the towns. While it is true that the urban birth-rate is beginning to rise and that there is a growing number of inter-ethnic unions, it is not at all sure that children born of such unions lose their ethnic identity. Even though family structures are breaking down, children still tend to inherit their name, status and ethnic identity according to the prevailing lineal system (usually patri-lineal). In rare cases there may be some street children who are ignorant of their parental origins.

In Chapter 1 we noted the concept of the urban host tribe. The host is the short-distance migrant who belongs to the ethnic group in whose homeland the city is situated. Hosts usually form the majority ethnic group in the city, which they may even regard as an appendage of their own ethnic culture. This may be the case especially with originally indigenous towns. Hosts are generally more amenable to urban culture and feel less threatened by modernization. They commute more frequently with the rural homeland and form liaisons more easily with people of other ethnic groups. Long-distance migrants from minority ethnic groups may form short-term unions with hosts, but usually prefer to choose a life-partner from the homeland that they visit less frequently.

Minority tribes tend to coalesce into alternative groupings in the city. These follow the patterns of cultural regions where adjacent ethnic groups have interacted historically and possess common cultural features. They are 'umbrella-tribes' or 'super-tribes'. In the homeland they may be more aware of their differences, but in town these become insignificant beside the dissimilarities of more distant tribes.[12] Ethnic villages occasionally come into existence where ethnicity is linked to a particular specialization. For example, the Luo tribe formerly working on the railways in Kampala had an ethnic village named after their homeland capital, 'Little Kisumu'. Generally, however, occupation of residential areas is multi-ethnic and neighbourhood is selective.

Urban networks

After the pioneering work of J. C. Mitchell in Central Africa, much has been written about urban social networks.[13] They are now a feature of town life in every African country. Networks begin at the horizontal level with equals doing favours for each other. Former class-mates or villagers who are not relatives socialize in town and form a circle of friends who are happy to help one another. The medical graduate obtains a bed in a maternity ward for a friend's pregnant wife. The friend is a banker who gets him a housing loan in return. The doctor also needs paint for a new house he is building. He has a friend in a parastatal organization that deals in building materials; this friend helps him, and so on.

The members of this circle keep in touch with their own families in the homeland. These relatives rely on them for help in their various difficulties, and especially for the education of their children. They help with school fees, board and lodging for those coming to town for study or medical treatment, contributions to the bridewealth required of young men wishing to marry, and so forth. They also have to find jobs for migrant family members. As a result of these demands, the members of horizontal networks find themselves at the top of vertical networks formed by their relatives. These vertical networks are further strengthened by clients who are not relatives, poor migrants who need a patron in town. In return for deference and small services, they expect protection and help. The system is strengthened even further when members of a horizontal network ask favours of one another for their relatives and clients, finding them jobs for example. It means that they are indebted to their new employer, as well as to their original patron. Furthermore, the process results in new horizontal networks of employees who help each other.

In African towns, networks are a way of life. They are also a major source of corruption and inefficiency. Finding jobs for clients and relatives results in overstaffing and in hiring unqualified staff. Doing favours for friends and acquaintances soon develops into exploitation and dishonesty. The cost of maintaining the network is so great that sooner or later the patron is forced to accept or request unauthorized commissions or bribes. Networks also have a political angle because through them politicians exercise patronage and build up their power bases. The power of a network cannot be broken merely by removing a powerful patron from the scene. There are so many horizontal and vertical links that it is virtually indestructible. Networks are at the exclusive service of their own members, ensuring security for them and making it possible for them to survive and to prosper in town. They constitute one of the most intractable moral problems of contemporary Africa.

In this chapter we have looked at the origins of the town in Africa and at certain features of its socio-economic organization. In Chapter 3 we shall take a more detailed look at the links that bind town and country in Africa, and the mechanisms that spread an urban social consciousness in the rural areas.

References

1 Stanley 1899, vol. 1, pp. 156–65, 308–9.

2 For Southall's typology, cf. Southall 1961.

3 Cf. Frankenberg 1966, who uses this category.

4 Oram 1965.

5 O'Connor 1983, pp. 28–41.

6 McDonagh 1986, p. 76.

7 *Gaudium et Spes*, 54.

8 Mumford 1961.

9 Dewey 1970.

10 Kubai 1985.

11 O'Connor 1983 (1986), pp. 139–42.

12 In Kenya, examples of 'super-tribes' are the Kalenjin, the Abaluhya and the Mijikenda.

13 Clyde-Mitchell 1969. This section is based mainly on Joinet 1985.

3

Peri-urbanization in Africa

The mushroom town

'Where is Musoma?' asked the Italian road-builder. The sarcasm was glaring, since the road he was constructing was intended to link the Tanzanian lakeside towns of Mwanza and Musoma. The tarmac had reached Magu, some thirty miles from Mwanza, and we were sitting over a cup of coffee there, speculating about progress over the remaining fifty miles of road. Headway was slow, due to lack of fuel, diversion of subsidies, and theft of materials. In the event, the work took another five years—at the rate of ten miles of road per year. The road was an important one and carried a great deal of traffic. It was the Germans who founded Mwanza in the 1890s as the southern port of Lake Victoria. When the British took over Tanzania (then Tanganyika) as a mandated territory after the First World War, they linked Mwanza to the rail and road networks. Musoma also developed as a subsidiary port on the western shore of the lake.

Not only did the Mwanza–Musoma road carry buses and lorries plying between the two towns, it also carried longer-distance traffic destined for the Kenya border farther north. Some of this was through transport to the East African coast from the landlocked states of Rwanda and Burundi, as well as from Tanzania itself. Some of it was tourist transport destined for the Serengeti and Ngorongoro National Parks. All in all, the Mwanza–Musoma road was a vital link in the East African transport and communications system, and Magu was one of a number of humble staging-posts along that route. In the early 1970s Magu was a simple stopping-place at a bend in the road

34

where a few kiosks and stalls offered refreshments to bus passengers and lorry drivers. As the road became busier, Magu thrived.

A cotton ginnery was established nearby and provided employment for fifty or sixty people. Then two local entrepreneurs set up businesses there. Both installed garages and petrol stations, as well as bars, lodging-houses and fine private dwellings for themselves. Next, a market for farm produce developed, followed by shops and lodging houses. Finally, the government decided to make Magu the headquarters of a new district. A regional trading centre was established for the distribution of commodities, followed by a district office, post office, police station and bank. A government housing estate was built and a small district hospital staffed by one doctor. Finally, in 1979, the Catholic parish centre, which for twenty-three years had been located at Kahangala four miles away, was moved to new buildings at Magu.

By the early 1980s, when I met the Italian engineer, Magu had 10,000 inhabitants. By 1990, the population had nearly doubled. Most of the business community are people with capital from more prosperous regions of Tanzania. People come to sell their farm produce and for other small trading and shopping. Young people make apprentice contracts for tailoring, carpentry, masonry and so on. Others find casual labour. The lodging houses, bars and discos are full of travellers, traders, government officers and teachers. For many, Magu is a stepping-stone to better and more secure employment in either Mwanza or Musoma, and these towns are stepping-stones in their turn to opportunities in Dar es Salaam, the capital.

There, in a nutshell, is the way in which urban consciousness spreads in Africa. The big cities put out tentacles. Opportunities for trade and income generation are created along the lines of communication, and migration begins. A rural bus-stop becomes a district headquarters township in a matter of years. The multiplication of such mushroom towns is part of the phenomenon we call peri-urbanization.

The city's rural hinterland

In Chapter 1 we discussed the so-called rural–urban continuum. One of the consequences of this phenomenon is the fact that cities in Africa acquire a rural hinterland of their own. This is peri-urbanization in the strict sense. From this urban 'periphery' derive two further instances of peri-urbanization in the wide sense. One can move outwards to the rural areas and note the way in which the city influences or urbanizes them. In this sense the city's periphery probably embraces

35

the whole country and it is this influence that encourages the growth of the mushroom town. Alternatively, one can move inwards towards the city's own centre and note the way in which rural values and practices are imported by the migrants. This is *rus in urbe*, urban living in a rural way. We shall consider each of these aspects of peri-urbanization.

Because of urban planning and expansion, city boundaries are drawn in such a way as to include much of the city's rural hinterland. In any case, African towns and cities attract a genuine village growth at their periphery. These are mostly villages of the host ethnic group. Being functionally related to the city, they expand with it, and are eventually swallowed up by it. The village hinterland also contains food plots and allotments farmed on a temporary basis by migrants of other ethnic groups. Often these are found in the as-yet-unclaimed areas, or areas awaiting development or settlement. Sometimes they are marshy, or unsuitable in other ways for building. So they become 'squatter farms'.

These villages and farm plots on the outskirts of African towns are crucial to the survival of the city. They provide a large proportion of the meat and vegetables consumed by the urban population. These foodstuffs are transported into the city for sale in the wholesale markets, or for immediate retail in the urban kiosks and vegetable stalls. Most of this production belongs to the small-scale, informal sector. Its importance can be gauged when there is a drought and crop yields on the city's periphery are low. Food shortages may precipitate out-migration to the rural areas. Not only is there insufficient food for urban dwellers, but stallholders lose their livelihood as well. In normal circumstances the local host-tribe derives an important income from provisioning the city in this way, and this boosts agriculture on the urban periphery. Cities in Africa are good for local farmers.

Long-distance urban migrants also go in for farming on the edge of the city. They tend to grow staple crops that require little attention. A favourite in East Africa is *sukuma wiki* (literally 'to last out the week'), a green vegetable that grows easily and is almost a weed. The long-distance migrant, however, is at a disadvantage compared with a farmer of the local host-tribe. He finds it difficult to patrol his plot and defend it against thieves. Farming the periphery is a useless occupation if the growing crops cannot be safeguarded from pilferers.

The town's rural hinterland attracts migrants who cannot afford urban housing or who seek an urban clientele without forfeiting their rural life-style. These include traditional doctors, diviners and mediums, as well as those who exercise traditional rural crafts that depend on the availability of raw materials, such as clay, skins, wood, bark, reeds or bamboo. People who live in these areas can also make a living by selling their produce and artefacts to travellers on the buses and lorries that ply the city's approach roads. Nowadays, some deliberately cater for the tourist trade.

The rural village in town

Illegal squatters are forbidden to construct permanent buildings, but they may be allowed to put up temporary or semi-permanent substandard housing. More rarely this type of housing may also be allowed in the case of legally settled low-income residents. In either case, rural housing models may be reproduced and rural materials used. Wattle and daub structures with thatched roofs are preferable to shanties constructed of pieces of rubbish. Thus it comes about that in many African towns low-income housing follows a rural style. Even approved permanent buildings may have more in common with the kinds of permanent housing found in rural villages.

Rural-type housing, however, is all very well in the spacious and relatively unpolluted environment of the countryside. It is quite inconsistent with the high population density characteristic of towns. Water supply, sanitation and rubbish disposal are only a few of the problems encountered, to say nothing about questions of security, road traffic and other hazards to life or health. 'Village' structures, such as wooden food kiosks and market stalls, are constantly springing up on the pavements of African city centres and in the shadow of prestigious, storeyed buildings. In fact, a constant war is waged against them by the municipal authorities, and they are continually being dismantled or moved.

If housing is rural, the people's life-style also has a rural flavour. In African urban areas there is much of the farmyard. Who, on his or her first morning in Nairobi, Kinshasa, Lagos or Accra, has not been woken by the sound of the cockcrow? Town dwellers in Africa keep chickens as they have been accustomed to do back home in the villages, and the buses and other public vehicles transport live poultry to town. Urban poultry farming is one thing, raising larger livestock in town is another. It is obviously difficult to find pasture for cows, though cattle are frequently found on the urban periphery, and cows are driven through urban thoroughfares to markets and slaughterhouses. Goats, on the other hand, are known to be unfastidious in their feeding habits, and they are frequently encountered in the low-income areas of African towns. They browse on the verges, hedges and river banks of the city and also forage in the middens and rubbish tips. Although it is said that urban goats are partial to plastic and that they are even traffic conscious, owners of herds prefer to employ a child to look after them and find grazing for them. Not surprisingly, the flesh of the urban goat is said to be of a lower quality than that of its rural counterpart.

In some low-income areas of African cities residents have a small plot of land that they can cultivate, and one finds paw-paws, cassava, tubers and squashes growing between the houses. Sometimes even the grass verges between the settlements and the main roads are planted out with maize or beans. 'Scratch an African', it is said, 'and you will find a farmer.' Even the urban squatters like to be growing things, if there is sufficient space. As in the villages, urban dwellers in Africa brew their own beer and distil—often illicitly—their own alcohol.

Mention has already been made of the survival, and indeed importance, of ethnic rituals in African towns. In fact, much of rural social life survives, particularly in the areas of greater social cohesion. These are especially the squatter and lower-income areas. This phenomenon is reinforced by the fact that new migrants from the rural areas form a substantial element in such localities. Many traditions of rural life appear to thrive in the African town and traditional explanations find new fields of application there. Communitarian rituals, however, are less in evidence than the individualistic power rituals of witch-finding and witchcraft accusation.[1] These reflect patterns of conflict and inter-ethnic enmity which are aggravated by urbanization and heightened by intense competition for jobs, plots and housing. The need for success in training, in examinations, in interviews and in business generally may also be worked out in these terms. There is also a constant preoccupation with security and health.

A striking example of traditional rural thinking in a modern African city occurred in Kampala in the early 1970s. It was at the height of Idi Amin's murderous regime when the citizens might well have had other preoccupations. Driving into the city centre one afternoon, I found the main shopping street and adjacent roads jammed by a huge crowd which the police and military were attempting vainly to disperse. I asked a passer-by for an explanation and was told that it was a case of witchcraft. The story was that a man had returned to his home above one of the shops in central Kampala and had caught his wife in flagrant dereliction with her lover. Being possessed of magical powers, the cuckold immediately bewitched the adulterous pair. It was alleged that the result of the spell was such that the guilty couple were paralysed, as it were, in the act of copulation and unable to separate. I returned to my residence on the outskirts of the city and on the following day read about the happening in the English-language newspaper. The reporter, writing no doubt for a readership that included foreigners like myself, poured scorn on the whole story. I reflected that, if the whole affair was an unfounded rumour, it was even more remarkable that it should have brought an entire modern city centre to a standstill and should have defeated the forces of law and order. Such is the power of traditional ideas in Africa over the most modern of cities.

The private work sector of an African city includes various forms of traditional self-employment. Many of these are concerned with one or another aspect of healing. In 1968 Lloyd Swantz found that there were some 700 traditional diviners at work in Dar es Salaam, sharing more than 10,000 consultations between them every day. Some 60 per cent of these were concerned with witchcraft accusation.[2] In 1971 Peter Rigby and Fred Lule, researching in Kampala, found highly organized and successful diviner-mediums who adapted their concepts and apparatus to suit the stresses and conditions of urban life.[3] New familiar spirits had been discovered or adapted from Christianity to personalize modern situations. Moreover, procedures had been streamlined to cater for busy city clients, many of them wealthy businessmen and government officials. Peri-urbanization, it seems, serves even the elite.

Traditional rural patterns of thought among urban migrants can also be discerned in the interests of town-dwelling Christians. The popular cult among Catholics of St Jude, apostle and patron of hopeless causes, is no doubt a somewhat ambiguous trend in the eyes of the better-instructed clergy and laity. However, it offers a useful case in point. Petitions lodged at the apostle's shrine in Nagulu, Kampala, demonstrate a predominance of vitalistic concerns. A sample taken in 1974 showed that petitioners were preoccupied with health, success, marriage, having children and promoting the welfare of relatives.[4] There was no substantial difference between the interests of urban-based petitioners and those who sent in their petitions from the rural areas.

New migrants tend to preserve rural forms of social organization for a time. One instance is the sex-division of labour. The finances of men and women are kept separate. Women are expected to produce or find the food, and to prepare the meals. Wage-earning men have money at their disposal that they are unwilling to share with their womenfolk. Such traditions may lead to the break-up of urban households and lead to a determination on the part of women to go it alone by seeking a job of their own or taking up one or another form of self-employment. Sooner or later, therefore, the demands and pressures of urban life catch up with the new migrants, and urban socio-economic patterns assert themselves.

There is obviously a scale of 'ruralness' in African towns. The smaller rural township that we consider in the next section is more likely to possess a more thoroughgoing rural character than the primate city, since it is embedded in a rural environment and a rural economy. Yet to a greater or lesser degree the phrase *rus in urbe* applies to all African towns, whatever their size. This is because African towns are obliged to absorb a continuing influx of migrants from rural areas and because of their dual allegiance to town and country.

The urbanization of rural areas

The mushrooming rural township is evidence that African cities have an even wider periphery than their own immediate hinterland. There is a sense in which a whole country becomes an urban periphery and in which remote rural areas are peri-urbanized. The mushroom analogy is not, in fact, misplaced. The fungoid growth at the centre puts out unseen spores that soon fructify and become visible in smaller growths in the surrounding areas. Not all mushrooms are poisonous, but they propagate themselves in similar mysterious ways. One does not become aware of the process until they appear one morning on the lawn. The spread of urban consciousness is equally insidious. It may not be apparent until urban growths are generated and mushroom towns appear. In Africa there is a strong interaction, not to say reinforcement, between town and country. Rural people carry their traditional values with them when they migrate to town. The same migrants bring back urban concepts and norms when they commute to their homeland. Many African families and communities have a stake in both town and countryside at the same time. In the short term this exchange may be beneficial, but in the long term it operates to the detriment of the rural areas. The mushroom turns out to be poisonous after all.

When the whole of a poor country becomes an urban periphery, most of its inhabitants are marginalized. Karl Marx's description of world history as nothing more than 'the urbanization of the countryside' is probably correct. Urbanization as a social consciousness is an inexorable process. It is bound up with technological sophistication and modernization. It is also bound up with the colonial expansion that was the fruit of Western industrialization. In Western industrialized countries the quasi-totality of inhabitants is urban dwelling and the wealth generated by the town is more equably shared. African towns are dependent towns and they depend on a world economy over which they have no control. Originally they came into being mostly as outlets for the export of raw materials to colonial mother countries and as inlets for the import of foreign manufactured goods. At political independence, instead of developing an export-oriented industrializ-ation, industries for import substitution were created.[5] Imports had created needs that were now to be met by local manufacture. Most of such goods are in fact destined for the urban elite, and the factories that produce them are town-based. New products continue to be developed in foreign countries and new needs created. These have to be paid for in foreign exchange and African countries are ultimately unable to throw off the shackles of foreign importation. While the price of commodities for export has fallen, the cost of imports has risen.

The African town is therefore an instrument of subservience to an unjust world economy and it reproduces this inequality in its own national environment. It favours its own elite and it accumulates wealth, industries and services that are not fairly shared with the mass of the rural poor. On the contrary, it enslaves the impoverished majority, drawing them into the web of urbanization and encouraging aspirations that cannot be fulfilled. The urban bias in Africa is part of a larger Western bias that inhibits effective development and self-determination.

Agriculture and urbanization

Although urbanization is a necessary concomitant of agricultural development, urban bias can vitiate it in many ways. Top-down administration results not only in a commercialization, but also a bureaucratization, of agriculture. A class of urban-based supervisors, administrators and extension staff is created which operates out of the rural townships and is responsible to higher government levels in the bigger cities. These salaried officials are not, themselves, engaged in farming, but regulate the work of peasant farmers and control the marketing and processing of their produce. In addition, there are those engaged in the new processing industries sited in the rural townships. The new agricultural hierarchy and its bureaucracy have brought about a social revolution in the rural areas, changing patterns of settlement and methods of cultivation or stock-raising, and, in most cases, taking the power to make decisions out of the hands of the real farmers. Harrison is very critical of the situation:

> The prevailing, top-down style of government is an arid climate for effective grass-roots development. Policies and programmes are all too often framed without consulting the people, and so are much less likely to command the popular support that can help them to succeed. Press freedom is often restricted, and non-governmental organizations weak, so leaders are starved of feedback on the impact of their actions at grass-roots level. Civil servants anxious for promotion are not likely to blow the whistle if things are going wrong in their area. There is a vacuum of accurate information, making it far easier to persist with misguided policies, and mistakes take much longer to correct.[6]

Worse than that, the farmer aspires to join the urban-based salaried class himself, to become a bureaucrat or industrial operative, or simply to invest in urban enterprises in the local rural township (such as the building of lodging houses). The civil servant in his turn yearns for a posting in the bigger cities.

Urban bias makes it difficult to recruit and keep good staff in rural areas, usually devoid of all modern conveniences from electricity and running water to shops and cinemas. Rural areas are still openly described by civil servants with the abusive colonial term 'bush' (*la brousse* in former French colonies). A spell of rural service is regarded almost as penal servitude or exile, to be completed as quickly as possible. Staff morale and commitment are low, and turnover is rapid.[7]

Urban bias undermines not only regular development programmes, but also programmes of aid or relief in times of crisis. It results in a general devaluation of agriculture in countries that depend on it for their very survival. In spite of the introduction of agriculture into the school syllabus, education in the rural areas contributes to the urban bias. Parents and pupils regard time spent on agricultural projects as taken at the expense of more profitable forms of learning. It is not farming, but literacy and book-learning, that will win the student an urban salaried job. Education is an investment for the family, the door to material and social success. No matter what the drop-out rate may be in the earlier stages of schooling, the education system is by its very nature competitive and elitist. In fact, historically, schools were first introduced by the colonial regimes in order to train civil servants and public-service employees, and they still largely possess the same function. As townships mushroom in the rural areas, children (including the school drop-outs) are given a further object

42

lesson in urbanization. Many are drawn away from the farms to learn new skills and trades that will stand them in good stead as they spiral upwards to the bigger towns and cities.

The affluent urban-based elite also have a private stake in the rural areas. Most are building a retirement house in their ethnic homeland and accumulating farmland there. Many belong to the new breed of 'telephone farmers'. These are absentee landlords, living in the cities, who telephone instructions to their farm managers but seldom visit their farms. Farming for them is a subsidiary source of income, and not their main occupation. Telephone farming is exploitive and wasteful. Farm managers do not necessarily share the owner's interests and farm land is frequently neglected or under-utilized.

Exploitive agro-business may be as damaging as inefficient parastatal bodies or absentee landlords. It thrives on cheap labour and saps local initiative. Like the other forms of urban-based supervision, it contributes to an urban social domination and, ultimately, to the pauperization and proletarianization of the peasant farmer. The urbanization of the countryside, and its conversion into an outer periphery of the town, is thus a form of internal colonialism, by no means always as blatant as that of the Bantustans in South Africa, but nonetheless real. Whatever short-term gains the rural population may derive from urban migration and urban growth, in the long term the countryside is the loser.

The urbanization of Africa's countryside encourages an uneven development within and between families. It favours a system of patronage and networks, and also the rise of economic classes in a hitherto classless society. Families with an urban salaried member are at an advantage over others. They can pay for the education of family members, or dispose of capital for rural development and economic enterprises in the local township. Families without such help become relatively poorer and a polarization of rich and poor takes place. In this way, the inequalities and injustices of the world economy are handed down to the grass-roots level.

The first three chapters of this book have helped us to understand some of the mechanisms of urbanization in contemporary Africa, how it is changing the face of the continent, and what its ultimate human cost is. We have seen how urban growth is based on massive migration and how migration in turn is supported by the urban–rural continuum. In this chapter we have examined peri-urbanization, the overlapping of urban and rural values in Africa, and the spread of an urban consciousness and even an urban bias in the countryside. The typical African town dweller is the urban squatter. In the next chapter we take a look at the reality of urban squatter settlements in Africa. To a great extent the future of African urbanization lies with them and they, in turn, pose the greatest pastoral challenge to the Christian Church in Africa. Most of the remainder of the book will then be devoted to the African Church's urban pastoral commitment and the forms that this takes.

References

1 Swantz 1970 makes the distinction between communitarian and power rituals and points to the latter's urban relevance.

2 Cf. Shorter 1973, p. 41, quoting research by Lloyd Swantz for a dissertation presented to the University of Dar es Salaam in 1968.

3 Rigby and Lule 1971, mimeographed report in the author's possession.

4 Some 302 petitions to St Jude made in April–May 1974 were analysed by the author and the Reverend Expedit Kakuba-Kapia.

5 Harrison 1987, p. 54.

6 Harrison 1987, p. 63.

7 Harrison 1987, p. 64.

4

The self-help city

Hell on earth

'Fire in the Valley! Fire in the Valley!' It was after ten o'clock in the evening and I was on the point of retiring for the night when the shout went up. I glanced out of my window in the parish house at Eastleigh in Nairobi and saw an ominous red glow in the sky over the shanty-town. It was as if the night sky was alight. I got ready in a hurry and joined the priests and sisters for the short walk to the squatter village where the fire was raging. Mathare Valley is the most notorious shanty-town in Nairobi, perhaps in all of East Africa. It consists of a filthy water course meandering through a ravine, the sides of which have been quarried and eroded into cliffs and steep inclines. This ravine is densely packed with shanties and hovels made of every conceivable piece of rubbish, wood, cardboard, polythene and rusty iron sheets. Here and there are rubbish tips and scrap heaps that engulf the buildings, forcing them to merge with the junk and garbage out of which they were created. Everywhere there are evil-smelling open drains. An occasional street lamp casts a fitful glimmer over the appalling scene. More than 100,000 people live here in these inhuman conditions, without proper sanitation, water or electricity and, what is worse, without security.

The fire had taken hold by the time we arrived and a strong wind was driving it forward down the flue-shaped valley. The flames crackled and exploded, as shanty after shanty succumbed to the fire. Firemen were directing their hoses into the centre of the blaze. People were frantically trying to remove their pitiful possessions before the

45

flames reached their dwellings. Others were raking through the charred remnants of their huts for lost valuables, or quickly reasserting their title to a plot by re-erecting some sort of shelter even before the ashes were cold. Police officers wielded hippo-hide whips in an unsuccessful bid to stop thieves stealing from the unprotected property. And all this frantic activity was lit by the eerie glow of the runaway fire. I was reminded of a medieval hellfire scene, a canvas, perhaps, from the brush of Hieronymus Bosch.

I joined others in helping a woman who lived alone to get her possessions out of her doomed hovel. I guarded property while the owners went in search of missing children. I tried to make myself useful in the midst of the pandemonium, but there was little one could do except be with the people in their hour of tragedy. If heaven begins on earth, I thought to myself, then surely hell, or at least purgatory, begins here also. Towards midnight we returned to the parish centre and I slept fitfully after the night's excitements.

Next morning I went down to the valley to see the area that had been burnt down. It seemed strangely small by the light of day, and it was difficult to imagine that seventy people had lost their homes in this fire-blackened corner of the shanty-town. People were raking through the ashes, even laughing in the midst of their misfortune. Church workers and relief agents were already distributing food and blankets. More sinister, however, were the men who were busy measuring and surveying the site for permanent development. Many people stood to gain from a fire in Mathare Valley, the landowners as well as the thieves. Government, too, was unhappy about the squalor. In the 1970s there had been too great an outcry when shanty-towns were bulldozed by the city administration. Nowadays, the authorities were content to wait for a fire. These, however, were so frequent, always happening around ten o'clock at night when people were cooking their evening meal, that many suspected arson, although the conflagration was regularly traced to a cooking stove. The official view is that insanitary squatter settlements should be eliminated, and that squatters are themselves 'surplus people' who deserve no consideration. Yet unpleasant and inhuman though the living conditions are, it is even more inhuman to bulldoze or set fire to a shanty-town. The destruction of shanty-towns is frequently advocated in the name of progress, but progress merely takes the form of jerry-built rooms for renting which rise rapidly in the clearings and promise a financial profit for the landlords. When a shanty-town is destroyed, a human subculture perishes with it. For all their squalor and filth, squatter settlements represent a human cultural initiative, an urban subculture created by the poor themselves.

Housing and services

Some authors approach the question of shanty-towns exclusively from the point of view of housing and services.[1] In fact, the phenomenon goes far beyond the mere problem of material living conditions. Sociologically, the squatter settlement or shanty-town is a subculture, with its own structures, norms and values, and it is perceived by outsiders as such. However, housing and living conditions enter into the definition of the squatter settlement and are the basic reasons for its existence and special character. It is therefore useful to take them as the starting-point in our discussion of the 'self-help city'.

What distinguishes the squatter settlement from other residential areas is its insecurity, its impermanence, its illegality. Fundamentally, the squatter settlement arises because of the inability of municipal authorities to provide adequate housing for the huge influx of urban migrants and because of government controls that result in housing shortages. In African cities a few affluent individuals possess high-quality private housing. Other high-quality housing is government-owned or private employer-owned. In addition, there is a good deal of low-quality housing owned by government and private employers, much of it dating from the colonial period. This type of housing often goes with a job. Since independence, foreign and local investment has helped to create a number of permanent housing estates in many African cities, for the benefit of lower income residents, many of whom have access to housing loans. Such forms of housing are beyond the reach of recent migrants, many of whom are jobless or casually employed, and who constitute the largest group of urban dwellers.

Those who cannot afford the high cost of permanent housing go to the shanty-towns. The intra-city settlements are preferred by new migrants who are seeking work or who are obliged to walk to their new-found jobs. When they can afford it, they tend to move out to the peripheral settlements which are linked to the city centre by the bus routes. Municipal bye-laws and government controls on leasing, on housing materials and on provision of services have much to do with the development of shanty-towns.[2] Behind the concern for maintaining standards of housing and hygiene lies an anti-migrant legislative tradition. This tradition has been inherited from colonial regimes that created racially zoned cities and that assumed that the rural African poor had no place in the urban scene. In some cases, an attempt was even made to control migration through pass laws. Because of the white settler presence in East and Central Africa, government controls have tended to be more pervasive there than in West Africa. The combination of less stringent controls and the indigenous urban tradition has meant that the squatter problem has been less acute in West Africa. In South Africa, on the other hand, the apartheid regime, which deploys far greater material resources, has pursued a relentless policy of moving spontaneous African settlements to government-controlled, higher-grade townships in conformity with the infamous Group Areas Act. Yet even there, it has not succeeded in eliminating squatter settlements entirely.

Government policy creates squatter settlements in other ways. For example, when a city boundary is extended to include the peripheral rural villages, these may be immediately reclassified as substandard. Types of housing and services that are tolerated in the rural areas are regarded as unsuitable for a town, and the villagers who built their own dwellings perfectly legally now find them declared illegal and perhaps threatened with demolition and redevelopment. In this way, peri-urban villages are absorbed into the squatter phenomenon. The squatter settlement differs by definition from the slum properly so-called, in its impermanent and spontaneous character, the term 'slum' being usually applied to deteriorating and sub-standard permanent housing. Africa, of course, is not without its slums in this sense. In fact, very often the older low-income housing estates have been invaded by poor migrants, and houses and flats have been turned into rooms for renting or multi-family apartments. As fast as new housing estates are built, older ones deteriorate into slums in the strict sense.

The squatter settlement is typically a 'shanty-town', that is, a collection of impermanent dwellings made of recuperated waste materials. Shacks or shanties are built of wooden packing cases, flattened kerosene tins, plastic board, cardboard, and indeed any serviceable item of refuse. In some cases, where there is an imminent threat of being bulldozed by the municipal authorities or burnt out by developers, people have been known to erect polythene tents which can be quickly put up at night and dismantled in the morning. To spend time and money on beautifying a shanty is impractical when there is no security of tenure. Where the surface area of the squatter village is limited, as in Nairobi's Mathare Valley, shanties are huddled together without designated plots and constitute a fire hazard and health risk. In East Africa's largest shanty-town, Manzeze in Dar es Salaam (Tanzania), there is more space available for building, but the area owes its squatter character mainly to the failure of government to survey plots and supervise construction. Surveyors cannot keep pace with the influx of migrants. In spacious Lusaka (Zambia), on the other hand, where smaller populations are involved, the shanties of Kalingalinga are set in numbered plots, with tiny gardens between them.

A characteristic of shanty life that is, perhaps, unexpected is that most shanty dwellers are tenants, paying rents to landlords for their hovels. Many of the owners actually live in the area and practise a small-scale landlordism. In Mathare Valley squatters clubbed together to buy land and form 'companies' or landowning associations. However, they were quickly bought out by wealthy individuals who lived elsewhere. In Kibera squatter village, also in Nairobi, most of the squatter land has been acquired by politicians and government employees.[3] Resident landowners are usually more insistent that rents be paid promptly and they are often ruthless in evicting tenants who cannot pay up. This is because their income derives wholly or largely from the rents they collect. Absentee landlords tend to exert less pressure on tenants, but, unless they enjoy political influence, they may be penalized in an upgrading process. This is what happened in Lusaka where the tenants were evicted and the houses owned by absentee landlords were demolished.[4] Absentee landlords are also suspected of employing arsonists to clear the shanties for more profitable development, as was hinted at the beginning of this chapter. One of the worst examples of profiteering landlordism is provided by Kisenyi, the squatter area in Kampala. Such problems, however, are less evident in West African squatter towns where ownership is more egalitarian and owner occupancy more common.

Landlordism invades even the imaginative site and service schemes through which governments seek to upgrade the squatter areas. In these schemes—Dandora in Nairobi, for example—plots with water and drainage are allocated on a random basis. The allottee is allowed to build in accordance with certain specifications and loans are given that can be repaid later from rents. In fact, the rules are very often flouted from the outset. Large numbers of people pay considerable sums to enter the allocation process. If they do not actually pay bribes to influence the result, they do so at a later stage in order to construct illegal buildings for increased profit. The promised loans may be withheld indefinitely, and ultimately, the allottees are defenceless when powerful outside interests move to buy them out. The occupiers end up by paying rent to absentee entrepreneurs.

If the huge influx of migrants makes the provision of adequate housing impossible, the supply of services is equally difficult. Squatter areas are densely populated and if the residents are politically organized, they can sometimes exert pressure on the authorities to provide a minimum of services. This happened in Mathare Valley, Nairobi. The municipal authorities may also be afraid that the squatter areas can become a health risk to other residential areas in the city. Water stand-pipes may be provided for people to buy a daily ration of clean water. Public toilets are often built and maintained, and perhaps a rudimentary open drainage system. In Mathare Valley the numbered toilets are the principal points of reference when a visitor is looking for a particular household. Some desultory street lighting may also be provided. Refuse collection is a problem. This is because many shanty-towns are literally rubbish-tips and may actually be called such. This is the meaning of 'Korokocho', for example, in Nairobi. Shanty dwellers live with rubbish and, to some extent, depend on it for building materials. Street children even scavenge the refuse heaps for food or saleable items of scrap. Generally, it is the lack of services, as much as the inadequacy of housing, that creates the inhuman living conditions of the African shanty-town. Improvement can only come about if authorities are prepared to tolerate squatting in greater measure, if laws are relaxed and cheap building materials are made available for more permanent, and preferably owner-occupied, housing.

The morbid factors of slum dwelling

Since squatter areas are already illegal by definition, it is hardly surprising that they are the focus for illegal activities. Some of these activites are simply a means of survival; others are an intended short-cut to the pleasures of affluent city life. While there is no doubt that a large proportion of squatters are engaged in illegal activities in the general course of everyday living, the professional criminals aspire to a life-style no longer compatible with life in the shanty-town. The latter may provide cover when men are on the run from the police, but it is probably not their normal sphere of action. In the squatter areas crime and delinquency are mostly prompted by economic motives. Petty theft is common, as is drunkenness fuelled by the illicit distilling of spirits. Alcohol has always been the refuge of the desperate and the destitute, and there is a constant demand for it. Drunkenness, too, is commonly associated with violence and sexual misdemeanours.

In the squatter areas there is similarly a market for drugs. These are usually obtained fairly cheaply and drug-taking includes the smoking of marijuana (bhang or Indian hemp), a traditional form of drug-taking in the African village, *q'at* or, in Swahili, *miraa*, a light stimulant that is also home-grown, and the sniffing of petrol, rubber solution and other forms of glue. Drug-taking and drug-peddling are also related to crimes of violence. Hard drugs, like heroin, cocaine or opium, are rarely found in the African slums, since they are expensive imports, but they can be resorted to by professional criminals who can afford them and who may be in contact with international drug-smugglers.

Prostitution of women and children is one of the commonest ways of making a living in the slums. The preponderance of male migrants, the need for female economic independence, the phenomenon of street children and the reality of crowded living conditions all favour it. The absence of normal family relationships and the morally disorienting experience of the shanty-towns favour sexual promiscuity. This also means that the incidence of sexually transmitted diseases is high. Today, as we noted in Chapter 1, these include HIV infection and the disease AIDS. Theoretically, prostitutes are both vulnerable to infection and instrumental in its bilateral transmission; however, it is notoriously difficult to assess the extent of HIV infection and the prevalence of AIDS in Africa. Clarke guesses that around 33 per cent of African city populations is HIV infected.[5] Yet this is not notably higher than the rate of infection in African rural areas. Estimates of the degree of HIV infection among urban prostitutes are high. In Nairobi, for example, infection among prostitutes has increased from 65 per cent in 1985 to 85 per cent in 1987.[6]

The difficulty in assessing the AIDS potential of African urban populations is the result of many factors: official sensitivity, incomplete case-detection, delay in case-reporting, and imbalances in the distribution of cases. The picture is further complicated by the urban medical scene, in which rural cases are treated in city hospitals, and where infection through contaminated blood products and injection equipment is possibly more likely. Because of the lengthy incubation period (up to ten years) from HIV infection to the development of AIDS itself, the detection of infection has been slow. For socio-historical reasons (discussed in Chapter 1) AIDS has surfaced in certain rural areas before becoming visible in the towns. Nevertheless, the disease mainly affects the younger, sexually active age levels, and it is difficult to imagine that the populations of squatter areas and shanty-towns will not be more seriously affected by the epidemic than those of the rural areas when the disease develops its full potential. On the other hand, there is evidence that the authorities are less reticent than they were about admitting and tackling the problem, and both health education and preventative measures may be more effective in urban than in rural areas. To this should be added the probability that the towns will learn from the experience of the rural areas. For the time being, AIDS programmes and AIDS prevention remain an urgent priority in African urban areas.

Mendicancy is another morbid factor in the African city. In fact, begging has been reduced to a fine art. Studies show that begging may be more lucrative than self-employment or casual wage labour.[7] A blind beggar was observed outside a shopping arcade in an affluent Nairobi suburb. Every time he netted a hundred one-shilling coins, he sent his boy companion into a shop to exchange the coins for a 100-shilling note. Enquiries at the shop revealed that the boy carried out this exchange some twelve times daily. If this rate were maintained throughout the year, it means that the beggar had an annual income of some £14,000 sterling. People with disabilities understandably exploit the compassion of passers-by in dramatic ways. Artificial legs are detached and bandages removed to reveal sores. Lepers sometimes veil their faces, however, leaving pedestrians to imagine the disfigurement beneath. Often squatters and slum dwellers put on tattered begging clothes and mobilize a 'family' of children to elicit sympathy. It is tempting for an unemployed youngster to take up a pair of crutches, rather than look for a job. Yet, not all beggars are confidence tricksters. For many, in the absence of a pension or a day-centre, a disability is their only asset.

Urban subcultures

Traditionally, urban sociologists have stressed the associative or network character of social relationships in town. This should not convey a negative or inhuman picture of urban social life. Recently John Gulick has been concerned to stress the humanity of cities against the anti-urbanism of many commentators.[8] He points out that cities are clusters of micro-environments and subcultures. Not only are there universal subcultures of class, ethnicity and life-cycle or generation, but there are also occupational subcultures and ghetto subcultures.[9] Squatter areas in Africa are culturally poly-ethnic, but there is a squatter subculture that transcends ethnic and generational divisions. More will be said below about the dimensions of social class, but the squatter subculture is defined in terms of how it is perceived to relate to the city or town as a whole. Squatters feel themselves, and are felt by others, to be extras, surplus people who are unwanted and rejected. They are portrayed as unproductive and as a drain on

52

the resources of the town. Squatter areas are regarded as dangerous, lawless places, the haunt of criminals and delinquents.

The affluent classes perceive squatters as a threat to their own security and living standards. They prefer to 'hold them at arm's length', at best to shut them up in distant low-income townships, at worst to 'sweep the dirt from the door' through forcible slum clearance and Draconian vagrancy laws. For their part, the squatters feel rejected by the city to which they have come, and the names they give to their shanty-towns are a humorously rueful reflection on a situation they are powerless to change. Korokocho, 'Rubbish Tip', has already been mentioned. In Nairobi there is also Soko Mjinga, 'Fool's Market', and Pumwani, 'Breathing Space'. In Kisumu (Kenya) there is Panda Pieri, 'Cover Your Behind'; in Kampala (Uganda), Shauri Yako, 'Serve You Right', and so on. The names given to market stalls, bars and kiosks are also part of this stoic squatter culture: 'Cloud Nine', 'Survival', 'Dream-Boat'. Even the brash mottoes and nicknames of the privately owned buses reflect the realities of the squatter outlook: 'Bush Doctor', 'Take Me Home', 'Your Lover at Service'.

The polarization of affluent suburbs and squatter settlements is aggravated by the juxtaposition of extremes of wealth and poverty in the African city and by the city's inherent irrelevance. As an island of wealth in a sea of poverty, the city centre and its affluent suburbs appear irrelevant to the majority of town dwellers. Much of this irrelevance derives from participation in the so-called world city, the world of international relations, travel and tourism. Airports, hotels, casinos and conference centres employ a fair number of people and bring in a certain amount of foreign exchange, but they are expensive to operate. They also serve priorities that are not those of the majority of the town's inhabitants, and represent a form of conspicuous consumption by rich foreigners. Investment in these things ultimately inhibits the provision of reasonable living standards for ordinary city dwellers. The development of African towns and cities is often geared to the needs of foreigners with standards of living beyond the wildest dreams of the ordinary urban migrant. Tourist enclaves are screened from unsightly slums or embarrassing beggars. The kiosks and market stalls that mushroom overnight among the prestigious downtown buildings are ruthlessly dismantled. Worse still, foreign criteria of investment and technological innovation are coupled with the architectural megalomania of some African rulers. Capitally intensive industry and foreign investment combine to maldevelop the town and to flatter and enrich the powerful few. Irrelevance aggravates polarization, the growth of violent crime and correspondingly violent repression. In the

53

Republic of South Africa where such polarization is articulated within a political system of racial discrimination and racially motivated social engineering, the antagonism between affluent white suburbs and poverty-stricken black townships is at its most explicit.

Considerable controversy surrounds the complementary concepts of 'underclass' and 'culture of poverty'.[10] The idea behind the terms is that, while certain migrants are upwardly mobile, improving their incomes and ultimately leaving the squatter settlements altogether, others are left behind because they lack education or other qualifications for advancement and are unable to avail themselves of the opportunities provided by welfare schemes. These sink into the poverty trap, unable to help themselves, isolated, rebellious, giving vent to their anger in vandalism and crime. This is said by some writers to constitute a culture or subculture of poverty with such characteristics as chronic unemployment, crowded living quarters, physical violence, early initiation into sex, and a sense of fatalism. On the other hand, while the urban poor are still in touch with their own ethnic cultures, and while the squatter settlement can be said to comprise a subculture in its own right, the forms of behaviour just listed do not really constitute a culture in the sense of an autonomous system of meanings. Rather, they are an assortment of actions and attitudes imposed on the poor by the rest of society. To some extent, they may be self-perpetuating in that they inculcate attitudes that discourage movement out of the ghetto. Whether they originate in society at large or among the poor themselves, these behaviour patterns are strategies for coping with deprivation and should not be an occasion for shifting the blame for their lot on to the victims.

Urbanization from below

Migration, as Andrew Hake pointed out more than a decade ago, is a form of self-urbanization or urbanization from below.[11] To this extent, the squatter settlement really is a subculture in the strict sense. The shanty-town is a 'self-help city', a viable system of self-reliance that initiates migrants to the urban mentality, offers services to the city, and constitutes considerable potential for urban life and development. When a squatter village is bulldozed or burnt to the ground, a whole way of life and a whole system of meanings and symbols is destroyed.

In the absence of housing and services, squatters create their own. They also evolve their own adaptive mechanisms to accustom themselves to town life. A substantial number of squatters find employment in the large-scale, formal work sector of the city, preferring to economize on their living conditions by eating well and sleeping crowded. One of the daily sights in an African city is to see the long lines of workers streaming out of the shanty-towns in the early morning and making their way on foot to the industrial areas and other places of employment in the city. Much of the traffic chaos in African towns is caused by the rush-hour exodus of squatters who take the buses, vans and lorries that serve the settlements on the city outskirts.

Many other squatters are self-employed in the small-scale, informal sector. A visit to a shanty-town reveals that every other dwelling houses a business of one kind or another: vegetable stalls, food kiosks, shoecraft, tailoring, shoe-shining, carpentry, stone masonry, tin smithing, radio repair, car-washing, photography, porterage, open air garages, traditional medicine, divination, handicrafts and, of course, the ubiquitous bars. There is considerable ingenuity in inventing ways of making a living or of supplementing incomes. To illustrate the spirit of initiative that pervades the squatter settlement, I will cite the cases of Samweli Irungu and Mama Maina. Samweli is a young man from Mathare Valley, Nairobi, who has taken up tin smithing. Every morning, in the early hours, he visits the local petrol stations and buys up their empty oil cans for a few cents each. These he carries to his roadside smithy where he cuts and solders them into the small kerosene lamps which are the normal means of lighting in the shanties. He can manufacture some thirty lamps a day and this brings him a yearly income of close on £2,000 sterling. Vegetable retailing is less lucrative for the middle-aged Mama Maina, but her business also requires an early start to the working day. Before dawn she makes her way to the wholesale market near Nairobi city centre, returning on the bus to the squatter settlement with a heavy sack of vegetables. This she has to haul down a muddy slope that leads to her dwelling, which also serves as a vegetable stall. There she prepares the vegetables for sale, tying them into bundles or sorting them into small heaps. She or her children then spend the whole day at the shanty selling off the produce until in the evening the stock is exhausted.

The squatter settlements abound with adaptive social mechanisms of every kind: ethnic welfare associations, cultural clubs, drama groups, sports clubs, literacy classes, informal schools, clubs in which skills such as sewing, typing or cooking are shared. It is in this area that churches and voluntary agencies have made the greatest contribution through the creation of community centres and through community building and 'functional literacy'—or the teaching of skills. In the final analysis, the self-help city is a positive instrument of urbanization and plays an integral role in the life and work of the city as a whole. It is very far from being a drain on city resources. On the contrary, it is a foundation that needs to be built on, not wantonly destroyed.

If the town is to be an effective channel of change and opportunity, one has to ask the question: To whom does it offer these things? Is it only to the affluent few, or is the underprivileged migrant included? Even though there is an absolute limit to what can be done to make the town safe, pleasant and healthy to live and work in, one can still ask: Safe for whom? Pleasant and healthy for whom? Standards of living for the affluent should not be so unreasonably high as to exclude the new migrants who are engaged in the process of self-urbanization, and who are as committed to the city as the elite.

In the next chapter we shall begin to look at the relationship of the Church to the town and its development in Africa, so that we can eventually determine the Church's role in the process. Our first task will be to look at the Church's approach to the urban phenomenon throughout Christian history. Then we shall take a look at Church and town in the history of Africa. After this, we shall consider what the urban mission of the Church might be and draw conclusions for the Church's own structures and ministry in the urban situation. Finally, it will be necessary to examine some of the special challenges and opportunities with which the African town confronts the Christian Church. In all of this, there is no doubt that both the growth of squatter settlements and the Church's own preferential option for the poor demand a Christian involvement with the people of the self-help city. As this chapter has shown, the poor are not only deprived people; they are people with values, with initiatives and with achievements of their own. Opting for them means entering their world, the world of shanties and rubbish-tips, of fire and health hazards, violence and insecurity. The Church has never found it easy to enter this world. Its ministers, who are usually drawn from the ranks of the non-poor, do not find it easy. But it is in the measure that Christians draw close to the poor that they remain spiritually open and creative.

References

1 Cf. Obudho and Mhlanga 1988, although they are aware of the limitations of this approach.
2 Cf. ibid., pp. 31–40.
3 Ibid., p. 32.
4 Ibid.

5 Clarke 1988, p. 182.
6 CAFOD 1990, p. 15, quoting Padian 1988.
7 Cf. Hake 1977.
8 Gulick 1989.
9 Ibid., pp. 183–217.
10 Ibid., pp. 196–200.
11 Hake 1977, *passim.*

5

Church and town in Africa

The City of God

As the traveller leaves the town of Iringa and strikes out towards the Southern Highlands of Tanzania, a large, rocky outcrop comes into view. Its summit is crowned with bastions, parapets and turrets, reminiscent of the mountain-top villages of Italy or the *bastides* of southern France. This romantic vision is none other than the Catholic mission centre of Tosamaganga. Its original 'citadel' or 'keep'—to pursue the fortress analogy—was built by German Benedictine monks at the turn of the nineteenth century. Their successors, Italian Consolata Missionaries, entered into the spirit of the project and lovingly completed it. Platforms, terraces and stairways link the various institutions that crown the hill: a boys' secondary school, a junior seminary, primary schools for both sexes, a fine twin-towered cathedral, houses for the priests and sisters, a training centre for lay-brothers, a catechist school, dispensary and maternity clinic, farm buildings, printing presses, workshops and outhouses, pumping engines, generators, garages.

A dozen biblical phrases spring to mind as one beholds this sight. This is the holy city, the city of God, the 'city built on the hill that cannot be hidden' (Matthew 5:14). 'Nothing that is impure will enter the city, nor anyone who does shameful things or tells lies' (Revelation 21:27). This is a glimpse on earth of the citadel of heaven, the great mission complex where the writ of God runs, not that of sinful humanity. It is a world apart, a total society, sufficient to itself, the realization of the theocratic ideal. The missionaries have long since moved into Iringa town, but Tosamaganga still stands as a witness to this earlier model. As such, it is only one example of the scores of Catholic mission complexes found outside the towns of Africa, crowning, wherever possible, a local hill. Peramiho, Kipalapala, Karema, Kwiro, Ntungamo in Tanzania; Virika, Nyamitanga, Rushoroza, Kisubi, Lacor, Rubaga in Uganda; Mukumu and St Austin's Nairobi, and Mathari in Kenya; Limbe and Likuni in Malawi; Chilubula and Ilondola in Zambia; Chishawasha in Zimbabwe; Marianhill in South Africa; Roma in Lesotho, and countless others. If Catholics had their 'Vatican Cities', Protestants had their 'Genevas' and 'Canterburys': Livingstonia, Likoma Island, Namirembe, Epworth, Kijabe and many more. The briefest perusal of an African church directory reveals that town-based parishes and stations are all of more recent date than those of the rural areas.

The anti-urban 'rural theology' that underlies this missionary history goes deep, and it is one reason why the Church still finds it so difficult to come to terms with the town. It is by no means a problem of the African, or missionary, Church only. Christianity as a whole has inherited a predilection for the rural areas and a legacy of anti-urban attitudes and images. When Christian writers, historians, theologians and apologists have written about the town, they have given vent to their pessimism. The indomitable open-air preacher Father Vincent McNabb OP was once asked to give his opinion about London, the city in which he had spent a major part of his priestly life. 'London?' he queried, 'You mean Babylon-don, my dear!' Babylon, rather than Jerusalem, was the favoured biblical image of the town. The ghetto Church, therefore, created its own uncontaminated enclaves, its own islands of holiness, away from the corruption, decadence and worldliness of the city. The missionaries who brought Christianity to Africa came with this anti-urban mindset. This mentality, together with other social pressures and historical circumstances that we shall examine in this chapter, combined to alienate the Church from the town almost till the eve of political independence.

The town in Church history

Anti-urbanism was far from being the stance of the early Christian Church. Indeed, the apostles and their disciples, most of them countrymen themselves, carried the Gospel first of all to the towns. In the apostolic and sub-apostolic age, Christianity flourished in the Graeco-Roman cities of the Mediterranean world. Christian communities were centred on urban households and family compounds.

The first places of Christian worship were private houses and the cemeteries that were the burial places of the martyrs. When Christianity was officially tolerated in the fourth century, the martyrs' relics were translated to basilicas erected in the towns by the Christian emperors, and these became the focal points for worship. The Christian *ecclesia* or assembly embraced the whole town and the liturgy was celebrated in the basilicas at different times. The bishop of the town and his *presbyterium*, or college of priests, would hold 'stations' in successive churches and celebrate the liturgy in them by turn.

Fourth-century Christianity was so urban-oriented that non-Christians were dubbed *pagani*, pagans or 'country bumpkins'. The few Christians to be found in the rural areas were assigned to the care of a *presbyter* or priest. The juridical terms *diocesis* and *paroecia* (late Latin *parochia*) were interchangeable and could be used indifferently for the town-based jurisdiction of a bishop and the rural community presided over by a priest. Eventually *diocesis* or 'diocese' came to be used exclusively of episcopal jurisdiction, and *paroecia* or 'parish' for the rural priest-led community. The diocese soon transcended the boundaries of the administrative capital and acquired a territory, the shape of which was determined by local political geography.[1]

In these early centuries the towns, protected by their fortifications, represented a measure of security and permanence, while the countryside was subject to violent vicissitudes as a result of warfare and migration. For centuries the rural communities were neglected by the town-based Church. It was not until the beginning of the ninth century that a systematic division of dioceses into parishes was embarked upon, but it was only in the eleventh century that the process really got under way. It was a lengthy and uneven process. In England, for example, the Domesday Book lists only 1,700 parishes at the close of the eleventh century. Two hundred years later there were five times the number. The originally rural concept of the priest-led parish was now suddenly applied to the town, and nearly every urban church was expected to have a territorial parish attached to it, with a priest in charge. Cathedrals, monastic churches, shrines, collegial or guild chapels all acquired parishes.

The systematization and extension of the parish structure in the rural areas was accelerated at the same time. Larger parishes were subdivided and all were grouped into archdeaconries and deaneries. By the end of the fourteenth century the process was more or less complete in both town and country. A few anomalies, however, remained here and there, and these were finally removed by the council of Trent in the sixteenth century. The reasons for this reorganization in both town and country were population growth, a new awareness of local identity, and the struggle against heretical movements such as the Albigensians. A tight, territorial parish structure ensured closer surveillance. A major impetus in carrying out the reform of Church structures was given by the Fourth Lateran Council, convoked by Pope Innocent III in 1216.

The fourteenth century witnessed a widespread demoralization associated with the towns. Not only were they affected by the terrible experience of the Black Death, but they were frequently besieged and sacked by the mercenary bands that roamed through Europe as a by-product of the Hundred Years War. They were also the abode of the hated Jewish money-lenders and usurers, as well as of foreign merchants who, like the Jews, were frequently victimized. The town acquired an evil reputation as a 'work of Satan' and a source of rampant vice. It was remembered that Cain, the murderer of Abel, had been the builder of the first city (Genesis 4:17). Early Christian images of the Heavenly Jerusalem and the City of God gave way to the biblical theme of the evil town: the cities of the plain, Babylon, Nineveh and pagan Rome.[2] The dualism of the book of Genesis, according to which towns were places of infamy and the pastures of the countryside were places of encounter with God, became the basis of a 'rural' or 'anti-urban' theology. Abraham's flight from Ur of the Chaldees and the destruction of Babel, Sodom and Gomorrah were emphasized, rather than the more positive urban images of the Bible.

This thinking lay behind the application of the rural parish ideal to the town. The rural parish, with its simplicity and homogeneity, became the model of church organization. In reality, towns were innovative places that threatened traditional social patterns. It was for this reason that anti-urban stereotypes became popular with intellectuals, theologians and moralists before and after the Reformation.[3] The guardians of society, the aristocracy of Church and State were also identified with the countryside, and the artistic taste of the ruling classes in the seventeenth and eighteenth centuries romanticized the rural and pastoral themes of classical tradition. The Industrial Revolution brought about a phenomenal urban growth in Europe and reinforced the inherited anti-urban stereotypes. To these were added Blake's 'dark satanic mills' and the grim poverty of Dickens's smoke-filled slums and pitiless workhouses. In contrast, Wordsworth and the Lake Poets proclaimed that nature was the guide and interpreter of the human heart, soul and moral being. Anti-urbanism has continued to enjoy a long innings and has even affected urban planning. The creation of 'garden suburbs' and then 'garden cities' in the twentieth century was another experiment in bringing the countryside to the city.

Just as the early Church ignored the rural areas, so the nineteenth-century Church ignored the towns. In Britain, Non-Conformists were quicker than the established Church (which had inherited medieval parish structures) in seizing the opportunity presented by the new urban populations, while the Catholic Church all over Europe continued to be identified with conservative rural communities. The eventual Christian response was merely to extend the urban archipelago of parishes, rather than to seek any radical new solution for organizing the urban apostolate. With hindsight, it has to be admitted that the growth of secularism in Europe had much to do with the failure of the Church to come to terms effectively with the massive urban growth of the industrial era. As we shall see, in Chapter 6, religious indifferentism is one of the regular hazards of rural to urban migration. It was only in the era of post-Second World War reconstruction that the traditional approaches came to be questioned.

Christian anti-urbanism in Africa

The missionaries who evangelized nineteenth- and twentieth-century Africa inherited the anti-urban bias of their contemporaries and co-religionists in Europe. Many of the sending missionary societies to which they belonged possessed their own spiritual enclaves, and it was in these closed environments that they received their formation. Maison Carrée, Hermannsburg, Herrnhut or Mill Hill were at that time rural retreats — liminal communities of future evangelists who, like Abraham, had taken the first step towards leaving their country and their father's home. Moreover, in addition to the experience of training, these future missionaries were seldom townsfolk themselves. The late Archbishop David Mathew, Apostolic Delegate to British East and West Africa, wrote in 1960 about the lack of Catholic missionary vocations from towns:

> The enemy of vocations, as also the enemy of Catholic life, is the great city. Even now the number of vocations that come from the crowded industrial areas of the great cities is very trivial. In this sense there is a resemblance between the body of priests of African origin and the priesthood of the old Catholic countries of southern Europe; both come for the most part from farming stocks and from agricultural labourers.[4]

The archbishop's statement is revealing, since it takes the city's enmity towards Catholic life for granted and draws an explicit link between vocation patterns among both missionaries and the African clergy they formed. The fundamental truth is that the early missionaries were farmers and that they felt at home practising agriculture in the rural areas. In any case, they had to do a fair amount of farming and food-raising to feed and support the inmates of their mission stations. Many of the latter were at first villages or settlements for freed slaves, refugees or other marginal people from among whom the first converts came. Usually they were run like collective farms or resettlement villages in which modern agricultural techniques, new crops and live-stock were introduced. The first missionaries had to be self-support-ing, so they needed to have 'green fingers'.

There were other reasons why the Church in Africa was rural rather than urban in orientation. There was very little in the way of an urban tradition in nineteenth-century Africa. Except in West Africa, indigenous towns were few, and missions were founded before the colonial towns came into existence. Missionaries depended on local chiefs for permission to start evangelism, and so their earliest stations were built in the vicinity of the chief's village. In West Africa, on the other hand, missionaries were sometimes obliged for similar reasons to occupy an urban compound, yet even in the west, they preferred to create their own rural enclave, if possible. When the colonial towns began to appear, there was no reason why they should grow up around the pre-colonial mission centres.

When the new towns of colonial Africa did begin to appear and to attract attention, they were perceived by missionaries as alien places. They were the administrative centres of a secular, colonial power. While missionaries could not forgo government approval, they had no wish to remain permanently under the eye of the administration. In some cases, colonial rulers were hostile towards Christianity, or at best uncomfortably impartial, favouring Islam, for example, as a counterweight to the Church. From a socio-economic point of view, Islam has always had an essentially urban character, and the adminis-trative and commerical communities of the early African towns were often in the hands of Muslims or other non-Christians. Ismaelis, Hindus and Sikhs, the indentured labour or immigrant business class from India, predominated in East, Central and Southern Africa, while the Lebanese held sway in the West. In the colonial period the largely foreign urban population was insignificant beside the massive African rural population, and both government and Church alike discouraged migration from the rural areas to the towns. The infant Nairobi, for example, was surrounded by a wire fence, and guards were posted to forbid entry to any African who was improperly dressed.

Missionary alienation from the town was reinforced at political independence. Missionaries, understandably, felt more uncomfortable in the proximity of African administrators than they had done in the presence of their fellow Europeans. It was felt that the African diocesan clergy should staff the urban parishes, and that they were better equipped to handle sensitive relationships with the newly independent African governments in their urban power centres. It was thought that clashes would be less likely to occur if missionaries remained outside the towns. In any case, missionaries prided themselves on being specialists in the rural apostolate, and the missionary role was essentially defined as one of primary evangelization or of carrying out initial apostolic tasks in marginal or remote areas. The 'fortress-missions' of the countryside were self-sufficient and could be maintained as long as people were prepared to make the pilgrimage to 'God's holy mountain'. Eventually, networks of out-stations were set up, and the attempt was made to give equal attention to everyone at centres nearer to their homes and places of work. Later on still, basic communities were started in many rural villages and Christianity began to be part and parcel of African daily life. The missionary prided himself on always going further and deeper, of penetrating to the furthest periphery. He was definitely not a prisoner of the parish office.

The rural specialization of the missionary was convenient, because setting up distant parish centres and out-station networks was a costly business. Building and roofing materials, transport, fuel and maintenance of vehicles and other equipment became more and more expensive, and missionary societies were better able to meet the costs through their own resources and through foreign benefactors, than through the local diocesan bursars. On the other hand, missionary ideals of personal poverty and abnegation also entered into the picture. Many missionaries felt guilty about living in town. The town was perceived as a comfortable place, reflecting the Western way of life that they had renounced. There were hotels, restaurants, cinemas, leisure facilities and other luxuries of town life which were felt to be out of tune with the Spartan life of the bush missionary. In Mbeya Diocese in southern Tanzania, the missionary bishop who lived at a mission station more than forty miles from Mbeya town was loath to move his headquarters there, but eventually did so in 1952. Even then, he forbade his priests from going to the cinema when they came to town to visit him at his new cathedral.

With the advent of political independence, there was a dramatic surge in urban growth. Between 1960 and 1980 the Church in Africa, despite an initial reluctance, and despite a lingering anti-urbanism, began to establish an effective presence in the towns.

The urbanization of the African Church

In the last quarter of the twentieth century it became clear that anti-urbanism was a luxury in which the African Church could no longer afford to indulge. Massive urban growth had changed the simplistic rural vision of the missionary. Moreover, the African Church had ceased to be a missionary Church. It had its own leadership and could set its own priorities. This was expressed in the years before political independence by the establishment of local Catholic hierarchies in almost every country, and by the appointment of Africans to leadership positions in all the Churches. This was a juridical change, removing jurisdictions from the control of missionary societies and placing them in the hands of African residential bishops with fully fledged dioceses. These dioceses no longer took their titles from the region, but now adopted the name of the principal town. Thus, the Vicar Apostolic of Upper Nile became the Bishop of Kampala; the Vicar Apostolic of Kilimanjaro became the Bishop of Moshi; the Vicar Apostolic of Kavirondo became the Bishop of Kisumu. The exchange of urban names for those of rivers, mountains and lake inlets was accompanied by the physical removal of the incumbent bishop to a town residence. Henceforward, the cathedral and diocesan offices were situated in towns and cities. Ecclesiastical administration, like its secular counterpart, was to be town-based.

As rural people migrated in ever-increasing numbers to the towns, it was seen that the urban apostolate represented an initial missionary task comparable to the primary evangelization of the rural areas. New strategies had to be devised for coping with the urban squatter settlements and the new housing estates. People from the rural areas were pouring into the towns, and priests, missionaries and church workers were obliged to follow them there. Urban parishes and chaplaincies for special categories of people had to be created, and new fields for specialized urban apostolates were discerned. It is instructive to see what happened in given instances.[5]

Dar es Salaam owes its beginnings and its name to Sultan Seyyid Majid of Zanzibar who started a small nucleus of buildings in the Arab style around the natural harbour and creek system in 1865–66. The German colonial administration revived the project in 1887, after

65

it had gone into abeyance at the Sultan's death in 1870. The Germans built their government offices and residential quarters near the Sultan's original site, and the British constructed a bridge in the 1920s to link them with the new high-income area of Oyster Bay and its 'houseboy village' of Msasani. A commercial area, dominated at first by Asians, grew up behind Majid's waterfront. Farther west again, and separated from the commercial area by a small park called Mnazi Mmoja, the African low-income area of Kariakoo (derived from 'Carrier Corps') was developed. The Central Railway, constructed in the first decade of the twentieth century, has its terminus near the harbour, and the city's main industrial area developed in the angle formed by the railway and harbour. In the 1970s the terminus of the TAZARA Railway from Zambia was also sited in this area.[6] Surrounding this nucleus is a mass of rivers, creeks, swamps and small lakes, and the city has spread over this entire locality, with middle-income and working-class residential areas on the higher ground and squatter villages in the less salubrious zones. Much of Dar es Salaam's squatter growth has engulfed the surrounding villages of the Islamized Zaramo people. Dar es Salaam expanded dramatically after the Second World War, when the harbour was enlarged and deep-water berths and anchorages were dredged, and new industries were developed in and around the city. Between 1950 and 1970, the population multiplied five times until, by the end of the 1980s, it was well over 1½ million.

The first Catholic parish to be established in Dar es Salaam was centred on the Cathedral of St Joseph, founded in 1889, two years after the Germans decided to revive the port and make it their capital. For sixty-three years it remained the only parish of the city. A Lutheran city church was founded at the same time on the harbour front, not far from St Joseph's. At length, after two world wars, Dar es Salaam's second Catholic parish was set up in 1952 at Msimbazi by the Capuchin Friars, together with a community centre and the Capuchin regional headquarters. Within six years two other parishes had been founded, Mbagala serving the industrial area and Oyster Bay located in the high-income residential quarter. These four parishes were doubled in the 1960s, as Christian migrants from the interior swarmed into the city and began to outnumber its original Muslim population. During the 1970s seven parishes were added, almost doubling the existing parishes yet again, and by 1987 another five. Today Dar es Salaam is served by well over twenty parishes, most of them in the squatter and peri-urban settlements that encircle the city.

Nairobi's story is much the same. The city originated in the angle formed by the Uganda railway and the Nairobi River in 1899 and a commercial area soon developed in the vicinity of the railway head-quarters. Houses were built for Europeans along the western approach roads, separated from the city centre by parks and open spaces. North of the commercial area, on either side of City Park, areas were set aside for Asian settlement. East of the river and along the north side of the railway an African township grew up and an ever-growing number of low-income residential areas. South of the railway were the railway yards and a huge industrial area. After political indepen-dence in 1963, the city grew rapidly. Outlying villages to the west were engulfed, and a number of squatter settlements appeared in the east along the Mathare and Nairobi rivers. Slum clearance for permanent low-cost housing has precipitated a 'leap-frogging' move-ment of the shanty-towns in a north-easterly direction. South of the industrial area and westwards along the railway new middle-income and low-income housing estates have appeared and more squatter outgrowths. At independence Nairobi had a population of barely a quarter of a million. In 1969 it was 400,000. Ten years later it had doubled. By the end of the 1980s it was well over 1½ million and on the way to the projected 2 million mark by the turn of the century.

The Holy Ghost Fathers were the first Catholic missionaries to come to East Africa, but until the 1890s they had confined their activities to the coastal region. In 1899, the very year of Nairobi's foundation, they founded the mission station of St Austin's, five miles outside the infant city to the north-west. Here they pioneered an extensive coffee farm. Five years later, the Church of the Holy Family was built on a site acquired in the commercial centre itself, and this was eventually replaced in the 1950s by the present Basilica, as the focus of a cathedral parish. Meanwhile, in 1922, St Peter Claver's Parish was set up near the Nairobi river to cater for the African population on the eastern side of the city. In the 1940s two parishes were founded in the Asian quarters of Parklands and Eastleigh, to cater for the growing Goan community. In those days, Eastleigh represented the furthest limit of the city's eastern expansion, and Nairobi was still a city of open spaces and undeveloped sites, with streets devoid of traffic. A former parish priest of St Peter Claver's once told me that he could clearly hear the parish priest of Eastleigh start his car two miles away!

For nearly a decade Nairobi remained with these four Catholic parishes, catering for the city's racial divisions. Then, in the run-up to political independence, the scene changed dramatically. St Austin's Mission sold off most of its land for high-cost housing development to the west of the city, but remained as a nucleus of Catholic institutions that tended, somewhat embarrassingly, to favour this 'European' side of town. Nairobi acquired three more parishes in the 1950s, four in the 1960s, five in the 1970s and six in the 1980s, as well as a colony of Catholic training establishments at Langata and Karen. By this time, Catholic structures reflected residential patterns and the density of population in the squatter areas more accurately. By 1989 there were twenty-three Catholic parishes in Nairobi, grouped in three deaneries, with seventy-four centres of worship.[7] The total number of congregations or centres of worship for all Christian denominations in Nairobi is around 800.[8]

A similar picture of the Church's entry into the city between 1950 and 1980 could be drawn for Kampala, Lusaka, Harare, Johannesburg, Lagos, Accra, Kinshasa, or any big African town. However, there was another aspect of urban growth that was equally challenging to the African Church. This was the rise of the 'mushroom' town in the rural areas. Regional and district headquarters townships are rapidly multiplying, and hitherto rural apostolates are acquiring an urban dimension. This is a development that will be treated at length in Chapter 7.

The urban relevance of the parish

In post-war Europe and in the theological discussion that preceded and accompanied the Second Vatican Council, questions were asked about the relevance of parish organization to the modern urban situation.[9] Since the parish is a territorial concept of rural origin, it has many limitations when applied to the situation of the city. There is a tension between networks and 'selective neighbourhoods' on the one hand, and subcultures and micro-environments on the other. There is no reason at all why urban parishioners should attend their designated parish church or Mass centre. Some would argue that the concept of a parochial territory is obsolescent as a principle for parish affiliation and liturgical celebration. In fact, the notion of purely personal parishes that unite individuals on the basis of rite, language or nationality has gained ground in the Catholic Church. Yet, even in the case of personal parishes, domicile is the ultimate criterion of parish affiliation.[10] Catholic canon law does not give parishioners a free option to choose which parish they will belong to. However, when all is said and done, the legal effects of parish affiliation amount to very little. Parishioners are obliged to give financial support to the parish of their domicile. Preparation for the reception of baptism, confirmation and matrimony cannot be undertaken without reference to the parish of domicile. For the rest, they can make their choice in the 'supermarket' of city churches, as the availability of public or private transport allows. For Sunday Mass and other parish activities, they can exercise a perfectly free option.

Town dwellers in Africa are notorious for changing their domicile and for moving from one parish territory to another. Frequently an individual becomes involved in the life of a given parish, in its pastoral council, its choirs, its associations and base communities, and is reluctant to give all this up when moving house to another parish territory. Short distances and the availability of transport mean that he or she can remain in the structures of one parish while living within the boundaries of another. In any case, ordinary parishioners have no idea where these boundaries are unless they scrutinize the wall map in the parish office. In Africa, the problem is further compounded by the urban–rural continuum. Parishioners retain a rural home to which they return many times a year. Consequently, they tend to belong to two parishes simultaneously, one rural and one urban. They receive sacraments in both, and this transience makes the keeping of parish registers, the organization of catechumenates and the holding of pre-nuptial enquiries extremely difficult in either parish. Weddings and funerals are often celebrated in the rural areas, not in the town parish. An urban parish may be completely deserted by its regular church-goers at Christmas time, when urban migrants return to celebrate the feast in the rural homeland.

Besides domicile, Catholic Canon Law also refers to 'quasi-domicile' and even 'quasi-parishes'.[11] Quasi-domicile is acquired through an intentional or factual three-month stay in a parish, while the quasi-parish is one that caters for specialist or transient communities, such as the academic community of a university, or the personnel of a military barracks. It has some of the functions of a full-blown parish. From all of this, it is easy to see how complex the question of parish affiliation can become for the African urban migrant. Furthermore, the concept of domicile or quasi-domicile as the basis of parish affiliation does not affect the work-place or work-orientation of the parishioner. Rural parishes are homogeneous or communitarian and rural parishioners tend to work in or near their place of residence. Urban parishes, on the other hand, may contain vast industrial areas with a daily influx of hundreds of thousands of workers. While pastoral work in these parishes may be conducted among a small minority of residents affiliated to the parish by domicile, the work sector may be hardly influenced by the Church at all. Many urban institutions draw their clients from parishes other than those in which they are situated: hospitals, schools and prisons for example. Then there are special residential areas, such as police lines, railway quarters, military barracks and university campuses, which require the service of a specialized quasi-parish. It is clear that the concept of the territorial parish requires qualification or modification in the urban situation.

Radical suggestions have been made.[12] One is to abolish urban parishes altogether and replace them with a presbyteral or ministerial 'pool of collaboration', a kind of super-parish or umbrella-parish for the whole city. Another is to create communities of celebration or Mass-centres which correspond as far as possible to the residential geography of the town, estates, tower-blocks or urban villages. Every micro-environment, according to this plan, would have its own designated pastor or pastoral team. Neither of these suggestions is wholly realistic. The Church, it seems, cannot dispense with the boundaries of territorial parishes even in the town. The least that can be said for them is that they have the negative value of setting a clear limit to the responsibility of the pastor. They can also be a framework within which to set up a structure of contact. Residential geography may or may not be a good basis on which to organize liturgical celebration, but it is open to the same criticism as the parish system itself, as being based on domicile. In theory, urban church attendance should not be a problem, since distances are short. The idea of a single pool of priests, ready to go anywhere at any time, might turn the ministry into an *ad hoc* agency, without continuous community contact.

In the next chapter we shall offer the elements of a solution to the problem of the urban parish. Inevitably, the aspect of territory has to be played down or transcended. The parish has to incarnate, in visible fashion, the Church's own urban mission. It will be the task of Chapter 6 to decide in what that mission consists.

References

1 Cf. Fliche and Martin 1959, vol. 12a, pp. 204ff.

2 Cf. Comblin 1968.

3 Gulick 1989, pp. 5–9.

4 Mathew 1960, p. 201.

5 The examples given here are more fully described in Shorter 1983a, pp. 26–35.

6 TAZARA is an acronym for the Tanzania–Zambia Railway Authority.

7 Downes *et al.* 1989 give the figure of 74 congregations, but they speak only of nineteen Catholic parishes. 'The Daystar survey was carried out in 1986. There is room for discussion about whether some of the parishes on the periphery (though within the city boundary) are 'city' parishes.

8 Ibid., based on the 1986 survey.

9 This discussion about the urban relevance of the parish follows that of Comblin 1968. Comblin's book, in fact, arose from the controversy following the Second Vatican Council.

10 Canons 107 and 518 of the 1983 Code of Canon Law.

11 Canon 102:2 of the 1983 Code of Canon Law.

12 Cf. Comblin 1968.

6

The urban mission of the African Church

A day in the life of an urban parish

It is 6.15 a.m. and dawn is breaking on the edge of an African city. It could be Kampala, Lusaka or Dar es Salaam. Or it might be Nairobi, Harare, Kinshasa or Lagos. City life slows down at night, but it never really stops. As dawn approaches it moves into higher gear. Long before the first streaks of light appear in the sky, people are rushing to work and bus touts are shouting for passengers. Streets are full of people and traffic. In spite of the noise and hurry, between twenty and thirty people find time to attend morning Mass at the Catholic Parish. They are mostly people on their way to work. Some are local tradespeople or stallholders, as many men as women. Perhaps, after Mass, the priests and sisters of the pastoral team recite Morning Prayer in the church as a small gesture of public witness.

Breakfast at the parish house is interrupted, as are all meals, by the door-bell: a cleaner needs keys, the night watchman has something to report. After breakfast, the parish secretary arrives and begins the daily task of entries in the registers, filling out baptism cards, typing up the correspondence. Then the community centre is opened up and the literacy teacher arrives to give his class. Later a women's group assembles for a homecraft session. At intervals in the morning beggars and refugees present themselves at the parish office. Some are sent to the diocesan refugee office. Others are given a meal voucher or directed to a Basic Christian Community for assistance. There is also a steady stream of other callers: parents who want to enrol their children for instruction, prospective adult catechumens, couples with a marriage case, parishioners who simply want to see a priest or buy a Bible or a prayer-book. The pastoral team holds a meeting to discuss the content of next Sunday's preaching and the visual aids that will accompany the homilies. After this there are visits to a hospital and a police station, following up some cases of injured people or people in trouble.

After lunch one of the parish choirs arrives to practise hymns and songs for the coming weekend. A women's sewing group is also meeting in the centre to make soft toys for sale at their downtown tourist kiosk. The schools are on holiday and there is a meeting of the vocation club for boys and the girls' holiday club in the afternoon. The congregation at the evening Mass is about the same size as in the morning, though women and children are more in evidence. Afterwards there is a meeting of basic community leaders with some of the parish team. As the light fades, the evening classes assemble at the community centre. Besides classes in accountancy, there is a classroom for students who come to study for their final exams next term. In the hall, the Parish Boxing Club is doing a work-out. Another choir is also practising. One of the Sisters takes Holy Communion to a sick woman on a neighbouring estate, and a priest goes to a basic community meeting in the shanty-town. It is 9.30 or 10 p.m. by the time everyone is back and the church compound is closed by the watchman.

This might be the shape of an ordinary weekday at an urban parish centre in Africa. The tempo increases, of course, at the weekends when there are many more liturgical celebrations, meetings and classes. Parish activities are endless: prayer-groups, associations, the catechumenate, meetings of the readers, ushers and lay ministers; the parish pastoral council, youth forum, Alcoholics Anonymous; opening of the parish library, the book-stall, sports meetings. The parish centre is a magnet for any and every kind of religious and social activity. In this chapter we shall try to discern the mission or final purpose that underlies it all.

Indifferentism and Church attendance

A recent urban Church survey suggests that urban in-migration in Africa leads to religious indifferentism.[1] Those who migrate to town tend to give up their Church involvement. The survey was carried out in Nairobi, the capital city of Kenya, in 1986, and it showed that while 73 per cent of Kenya's population claims to be Christian and 40 per cent actually attend church weekly in the rural areas, only 12 per cent of the city's population attends church every week. Occasional (less than weekly) attendance might reach 20 per cent, but the majority, 60 per cent, of the population never go near a church and only 4 per cent claim to be involved in Christian activities other than attendance at church.

Understandably, there is a considerable variation among the actual Churches in this matter. 54 per cent of Nairobi's Christians are members of the Catholic Church, but only 30 per cent of Christians who attend services go to Catholic churches. 4 per cent claim to be Anglican, but 8 per cent attend Anglican churches. Orthodox break even at 1 per cent membership and attendance. Indigenous Churches claim to have a 22 per cent membership, but their church attendance is 25 per cent of the city's total, while the combined membership of all the city's mission-related Protestant Churches (Presbyterian, Methodist, Baptist, Evangelical, etc.) only claim a 19 per cent membership but enjoy 36 per cent of the attendance.[2] The consolidated Protestant figure would have to be broken down before final conclusions could be drawn, but it appears that the Catholic Church is alone among the five categories in having more people affiliated than actually attending. As the report suggests, a major reason for this is the lack of church buildings or centres of worship and Church activity. There are only seventy-four Catholic worship centres in the city, compared with 330 Protestant ones. Catholic churches average an attendance of 2,324 people! Anyone who attends Mass in a Nairobi Catholic church knows how packed they are. In Eastleigh (including most of Mathare Valley shanty-town), for example, where the percentage church attendance is one of the lowest in the city and the percentage membership more than the average, the 10 o'clock Sunday Mass at St Teresa's Catholic Parish is regularly attended by upwards of 1,500 people.

The survey reveals that the low proportion of church attendance remains constant, even though the city's population increases at the rate of 500 a day. All the denominations are increasing their congregations and worship centres. During the period studied by the survey Nairobi's Catholic parishes grew from thirteen to nineteen, yet its share of church attendance dropped from 56 per cent to 30 per cent. Even to maintain the status quo of 12 per cent church attendance, Nairobi's Christian denominations would have to treble the annual rate at which they establish new churches or worship centres. Religious indifference is not correlated with such factors as youth, lack of education or unemployment. It is welcome news that African urban church attendance is not noticeably age-related. Otherwise one might have concluded that the decline was related to the youthfulness of the urban population, as it is elsewhere in the world. In Nairobi, young people, educated people and wage-earners are proportionately higher in the church congregations than in the city as a whole. The indigenous churches tend to attract the poorer classes, while the other denominations are finding it difficult to address the poor. Nairobi's sex-ratio favours men above women, and adults above children, yet women and children are over-represented in the city's church attendance.

It is necessary to consider the implications of a survey like this for the Church's mission in the African city. What should the Church be doing? What is the goal of all its activity? The survey in question was made by an Evangelical college,[3] and its interpreters assume that rapid numerical growth should be a major goal. This, in turn, depends on evangelism (or evangelization) conceived primarily as an exercise in communication or outreach. The survey admits that there are no simple answers to the problem, and admittedly evangelism and conversion work must be included among the solutions. Yet evangelism/evangelization is not merely a question of proclaiming a message, or even of ensuring a better attendance at worship centres. No doubt, Churches would like to eliminate unfavourable discrepancies between affiliation and attendance, and they would welcome fast Church growth if this also implied rooting the faith more deeply in individuals and communities. But ultimately evangelization means celebrating and living the Good News of Jesus Christ, not competing at all costs for Church membership. It means ensuring that Gospel values permeate societies and cultures. It means reconciling people to God and to one another, overcoming the barriers that divide Churches, classes and ethnic groups from each other. Finally, it means gathering people in the forgiveness of Christ, building a community that is the Body of Christ.

Churches should be worried if they are not reaching the poor and powerless with whom Christ himself identified and whom he upheld as true heirs of the Kingdom. Modernization, as we have seen, creates its own myth of material success and comfort. Its principles are 'reality principles': possessions, power, prestige, pride.[4] Modernization, by itself, militates against Gospel values and favours the growth of a secularism that is undoubtedly linked to the absence of a sense of God and a sense of sin. If urbanization entails the growth of secularism, then urgent attention must be paid by the Churches to re-evangelization as a missionary priority. Since it is a priority for the Western world as much as for Africa, and since secularism is everywhere linked to a West-inspired modernization, solutions have to be sought in partnership. Overcoming indifferentism, as an inevitable concomitant of urbanization, is certainly an important component of the Church's urban mission.

The urban parish as event

One of the conclusions of Chapter 5 was that the concept of the urban parish as a territory contained inherent limitations. It has been persuasively suggested that the urban parish should be regarded as an event, rather than as a territory.[5] The parish, to this way of thinking, is a happening or experience that draws people to it, as a source of stability, integration and prayer. The parish centre exerts a gravitational pull on its surroundings, but is not submerged by any residential area or micro-environment. It is a 'house of the Church' which beckons to people and welcomes them.[6] It is not only a place where the Gospel is celebrated in worship, but a place where Christians help the Church fulfil its entire urban mission. It needs to have a physical existence, not merely in the shape of a handsome place of worship, but in facilities for the community: a hall, a set of rooms, a community centre, a multi-purpose building. This is the place in which relationships are created, resource-persons trained and services offered. The parish has to be a source of reflection, prayer, spiritual growth, stimulation and renewal.

Since (as we shall see in Chapter 7) as much importance has to be given to interparochial and supra-parochial structures in the town as to the parish itself, many of the activities at the parish centre take place on behalf, or at the behest, of these structures. Services need to be co-ordinated for the whole city or for the deanery, and since the parish is not a self-contained unit, it gives material form to common policies and programmes. Parish centres, therefore, become venues for co-ordinated activities of all kinds: youth events, retreats, training sessions, seminars, sports fixtures. This supra-parochial function also helps to cater for those who move their residence from one parish to another. But the parish is not merely a magnet that draws people to it; it is also a rotatory mechanism that propels people outwards to other environments in the city, to their work environments in the first place, and to their various 'selective neighbourhoods' and networks. The urban parish is consequently very different in reality from the legalistic ideal of a static territory. Its action upon the city is simultaneously centripetal and centrifugal and its impact is more penetrating and elusive.

Because evangelization entails the breaking down of barriers and the gathering together of people in a community of faith, the urban parish is a centre of stability and integration. In the African city (and any modern city today) there are ethnic barriers as well as class barriers to be overcome. There are also barriers created by occupational differences, and the barriers due to differences of sex, age and education. The parish has to bring all these sectors together, and make use of the gifts and contributions of each. In this chapter we deal, in particular, with the ethnic and class barriers. In Chapter 9 we deal separately with the integration of youth in the parish community.[7]

The Church as social worker

The Gospel is proclaimed to, and lived by, people who are embodied spirits, and there is no way in which the Church can indulge in evangelism without subscribing to a social gospel. Spiritual values cannot be preached without practical involvement in the material everyday life of Church members. Evangelization necessarily has a social dimension, since one of its aims is to gather people into a community that is the Body of Christ. In particular, the urban poor experience in the Church the love of a Christ who cares for them in their bodily, as well as their spiritual, needs. The message of salvation is a message of integral human liberation and promotion. For this reason, the Church's first task in the city is to attack the latter's morbid factors and to help people improve the quality of their material and social life. It is relatively easy, perhaps, for the popular itinerant evangelist to address vast crowds without becoming socially involved. The pastor who shares the daily life of the urban poor over long periods of time rightly forfeits credibility if he condones or ignores the obvious social injustices with which he is surrounded. Yet, in helping people to improve their living conditions, care must be taken that a fundamentally unjust system is not made permanent. It is not enough merely to tackle the secondary consequences of urban growth. Structural injustice must be confronted at the same time.

The Church in the city tries to improve conditions through socio-economic liberation and change. Temporary solutions are adopted as a crisis measure, but always with the long-term solutions in view. People from the squatter self-help areas must be helped to acquire a share in the urban services to which they are entitled and which only a minority of town dwellers enjoy. This is a question of justice, especially since many squatters are integrated into the city's large-scale, formal work sector. They must be helped to improve their material and social life and to make this improvement an on-going feature. They must become aware of the ways in which their particular vulnerability is exploited by the wealthy and powerful, as well as by officials who abuse their authority. Through its social apostolate and specialist care, the Church in the city fights against disease, insanitary conditions, illiteracy, violent crime, drunkenness, drug-taking and prostitution. It risks unpopularity with the authorities by campaigning against injustice in the administrative system: corruption, intimidation, extortion, police brutality and so on.

Often the urban parish employs a full-time social worker to deal with the various categories of people who call upon the Church for help: refugees, homeless travellers, neglected elderly people, orphans, alcoholics, drug-takers, victims of violence. The parish team is frequently called upon to transport emergency cases to hospital, to help look for missing persons in police cells, remand prisons, hospitals or morgues, to find homes for abandoned infants or geriatric patients, to provide for families made homeless by fire or eviction. The list of cases in which individuals call upon the Church for help is endless, and many need personal attention from a trained social worker. Often the cases can be dealt with through Church structures, particularly through the basic Christian communities, if these are present in the parish. The parish team has to make a point of working with, and not merely for, its parishioners. Besides catering for emergencies, Christians need to be stimulated to increase their awareness of all the trends and factors that affect them in the urban situation. The parish enables them to take control of their lives.

Besides dealing with individual cases on a one-to-one basis as they occur, urban parishes create specialized social institutions of their own. Some of these are parish-owned. Other Church-sponsored organizations and movements operate within deanery and diocesan structures, or are even independent of them altogether. This independence favours freedom of action in finances and policy-making. An example of a diocesan social organization was the late Father Bart Fleskyns's Kampala Sharing Club which helps rehabilitate young offenders on their release from prison. An example of an independent organization is the well-known Undugu ('Brotherhood') Society of Kenya, founded by Father Arnold Grol in Nairobi in 1974. Undugu specialized at first in caring for the 'parking boys' and street children of the city, offering them foster homes and basic education units, otherwise known as 'schools without uniforms'. Undugu also started income-generating projects of various kinds: knitting, sewing, embroidery for the women, and co-operatives of artisans—carpenters, metal-workers and tailors—for the men. Special attention has also been given to the needs of handicapped children. Projects were started for them in which their parents were also involved. Educational programmes were devised to teach people management, book-keeping and marketing skills, and training centres were eventually set up to teach such skills as mechanics, carpentry, masonry, metal-working and shoecraft.

At various times Undugu has started basic health-care programmes, with special attention to immunization, first-aid, hygiene and nutrition. It has also created clubs for prostitutes to teach them legitimate, income-generating skills, such as shorthand-typing or homecraft. It has created other social, cultural and sports clubs for youth, and has even founded an agricultural college on an experimental farm outside the city in order to attract some of the migrants back to the rural areas abandoned by them. An important project has been the establishment of craft shops for tourists in downtown Nairobi. The income from the tourist trade helps pay the salaries of the dedicated local people who run the organization.

Many of the kinds of project started by organizations such as Undugu have also been attempted by parishes on their own. Sometimes they are helped by international funding agencies such as Save the Children, Help the Aged, Shelter and so on. In 1982 Undugu helped a slum community to rebuild 240 semi-permanent houses, and it was demonstrated that shanty dwellers will improve their circumstances dramatically if they can buy cheap building materials. In Eastleigh Catholic parish in 1988 a group of women started a building materials factory, to provide bricks and roof tiles for better-quality housing. Another concern of the Church is to care for the criminal casualties of city life by supplying books to prisoners and helping them take study courses so as to acquire qualifications useful for job-seeking when they are released.

The urban parish needs premises of its own, a compound to which people can resort, a hall for gatherings of all kinds, classrooms and offices, perhaps a fully equipped domestic science area. When such a community centre is set up, the local Christian community should be required to contribute towards the cost, so that people feel it belongs to them. They should be encouraged to use it freely and to see it as a place in which to feel at home. A parish may also employ specialist teachers on a full-time or part-time basis for adult education programmes of different kinds: literacy, book-keeping, homecraft. In the final analysis there is no limit to the possibilities of urban social involvement by the Church. In the African town, the Church becomes an adaptive social mechanism, helping new townspeople adjust to their changed circumstances and assisting positively in the process of urbanization. Through its social involvement the Church is one of the guarantors of social justice in the urban situation.

The Church and urban social integration

Virtually every Kenyan ethnic group is represented in Eastleigh Catholic Parish, Nairobi. There is a large group of Kikuyu from nearby Central Province and a considerable contingent of the neighbouring Kamba, as well as peoples from the Mount Kenya area, the Meru and Embu in particular. There are also Taita and Giriama from the Coast. From western Kenya, the Luo are the biggest group, and there are many of the Luyia and Kalenjin peoples, as well as Gusii. Each tribal group uses its own vernacular among its own members and some have prayer-groups which meet and pray in their own language. In church, however, the national language of Kenya, Swahili, is used for Mass and the sacraments. In a city like Nairobi, the diversity of languages is a fundamental obstacle to co-operation—and even sometimes to social justice. People are disposed to favour those of their own language group and to take little or no interest in the others. That is why, in these multi-ethnic situations, both Church and government try to emphasize the use of the Swahili language.

On the Feast of Pentecost 1989, Eastleigh Parish held an unusual liturgy in which the need for co-operation among the different language groups was emphasized.[8] As is the custom on great feasts, the principal Mass was held in the open air, in the parish compound, and was attended by more than 3,000 people. The compound was decorated as usual with banners hung from poles set up on the perimeter. A new feature, however, was that each pole bore a placard with the name of a tribe or ethnic group on it. As the Christians assembled for Mass, they were asked to gather according to tribe, around their own placard. Mass began and then the first reading from the Acts of the Apostles was read aloud in each of the groups in their own vernacular. Just as happened at the very first Pentecost in Jerusalem, each group heard the wonderful news from God in their own mother-tongue. Then came the second reading from St Paul about the same Spirit working in various ways in different people for the good of the whole community. For this reading, the groups in the congregation were asked to mingle with one another so that all the tribes were mixed up, and the lesson was read aloud by one reader in Swahili only. The Gospel then followed in the same, national language.

This liturgical experience made a profound impact on all the people present. In fact, it so moved the members of one tribe, the Kamba, that they decided there and then to found a Society of the Holy Spirit, to encourage their Kamba members to co-operate with people of other ethnic groups, to listen to them and to be fair towards them. For them and for others at Eastleigh, Pentecost really came alive that year. One of the Church's tasks in the city as an adaptive mechanism is to assist in the social integration of the various ethnic groups in a multicultural society. Although ethnic parishes are increasing in other parts of the world, they are generally not warranted in African towns. Both government and Church, with their policies of integration, frown on them, and they are only really demanded by the presence of new or transient minority groups. People are encouraged to safeguard their ethnic cultures, but also to make a contribution at the multicultural level, using vehicular or national languages.

It often happens that, because of a numerous following in a rural ethnic homeland, a given Church will be attended by a majority of that particular ethnic group in town. In Nairobi City, for example, the Kikuyu are the biggest group among Catholics, while Luo are more numerous among Anglicans. The Luyia constitute a third of both the other Protestant Churches and the indigenous movements.[9] Care has to be taken that a Church is not effectively dominated by one group, to the exclusion of the others. Although an excellent preparation for the African urban ministry is a pastoral experience in an ethnic homeland, the pastor must beware of identifying with this particular ethnic group. If possible, the pastoral team itself should cater for several vernaculars.

One of the Church's urban tasks, therefore, is to break down the inner frontiers that divide and exclude people. This is not done by denying the validity of ethnic cultures, but by cultural re-education, cultural development and especially intercultural communication within the parish. The aim is to convert cultural pluralism into genuine multiculturalism. It is not enough for ethnic cultures to be juxtaposed in close proximity (cultural pluralism). There must be a communication between them. They should coexist in a state of complementarity (multiculturalism). From experiencing other cultures with a certain degree of shock, people are led to co-operate in spite of the differences they experience. While there may be a measure of cultural loss, nevertheless cultural identities are maintained through dialogue and cultural interchange. This can even result in a measure of cultural enrichment.

Running a multi-ethnic urban parish calls for considerable tact and skill. One should not encourage people to sever their links with the rural homeland, but these links should not be emphasized to the detriment of urban church structures. Rural parishes and rural dioceses are not 'personal' in the sense that they have jurisdiction over their fellow tribesmen in town. The great value of the urban phenomenon is the experience of unity-in-diversity, of appreciating others in their difference, learning to receive from, and share with, others.

One field of social integration concerns the so-called 'suburban captivity' of the Church.[10] The suburb is associated with the affluent elite. It is a 'dormitory' or 'hotel without a roof', in which individuals and their families reside in anonymity and comfort.[11] The housing is of high quality and often surrounded by gardens. It may even be self-consciously a 'garden suburb'. In suburbia, ownership of private transport encourages 'selective neighbourhood' in its most extreme form. Families drive for miles to consort with a selected neighbour, without having anything to do with the people next door. Suburban living is both the cause and the consequence of individualism, with its limited ideals and short-term priorities. The garden suburb is even a subtle form of anti-urbanism, possibly of anti-culture, in which individuals incapsulate themselves in their own ideal environments. As such, it is frequently exploitive. People in the higher-income groups are in the town, but not of it. They try, consciously or unconsciously, to set urban realities at a distance.

The suburban parish is in grave danger of identifying too closely with its immediate environment, the suburb. What follows is the suburban captivity, or the 'bourgeoisification' of the Church.[12] The Church espouses the myopic interests of the affluent and cuts itself off from the mission of the Church to the town as a whole. In such a situation, Christians must be helped not merely to overcome the barriers that separate individuals from one another within the suburb, but above all to help them cross over the boundaries of suburbia itself. This is a case in which the strict enforcement of territorial parish boundaries actually inhibits the Church's urban mission. The Church has to help its bourgeois members understand how their own manner of living impoverishes and exploits others.

Salvation is offered by Christ to rich and poor alike, but within this universal salvation rich and poor are both obliged to follow Christ in his choice of poverty and in his preference for the materially poor. This is not to say that the rich are to become 'do-gooders' or 'Lady Bountifuls', condescending in their charity towards the poor in other parts of the city. It means that they must accept to be evangelized by the poor themselves, to listen to them and to learn from them. It means also that they have an obligation to alleviate the inhuman living conditions of the poor who share their city. They do this especially by helping to remove the structures of injustice that impoverish and dehumanize the poor. Above all, they are obliged to relate to the poor as fellow human beings and fellow Christians, to meet them on a basis of equality and friendship. It is always best if an urban parish (or at least deanery) unites people of divergent classes in both suburbs and slums. Oyster Bay Catholic Parish in Dar es Salaam brings together both the affluent of Oyster Bay and the fishermen and houseboys of Msasani Village. Even in Nairobi the high-class Muthaiga district and the squatters' Mathare Valley are found together in Eastleigh Catholic Parish. If such amalgamations cannot be achieved at parish level, then links have to be created at supra-parochial levels.

The urban mission of the Church

Theological anti-urbanism is unjustified. The Bible, it has been said, begins in a garden and ends in a city. In spite of the ways in which urban growth and urban social consciousness operate unfavourably towards the mass of the African poor, cities and towns have many strengths and positive social values. The Church's task is to enhance these and to counteract the adverse effects of population size, density and heterogeneity, as well as the harmful consequences in the rural areas of a socio-economic urban bias. As we shall see in Chapters 7 and 8, the Church does this largely through creating contact-structures and through basic community building. There is no doubt that the relative social cohesion of the squatter villages and their subcultures is an advantage and that the evangelization of the city as a whole can more easily begin from there. Unfortunately, the Church is still, in many African towns, subject to a suburban captivity, and is thus not disposed to receive initiatives from the slums or to welcome a Gospel preached by the poor.

My great-grandfather, Francis Caudwell, was an Anglican priest involved in the Catholic renewal movement of nineteenth-century London's East End. His ideal was that the Church should stand at the centre of human deprivation to proclaim God's glory. Street services and public witness took place in order to draw people to worship in the church building.[13] This was an ecclesiocentric vision of the Church's urban mission. Today, we think of the Church-Event, rather than the church building, pointing to God's dwelling among his people. At the heart of this people, God is present, sharing their struggles and their hopes. Through their mouths, and with their voices, God speaks to the world. Church organization, church buildings and church services exist to bring about a realization of this divine tent-dwelling.

The goal is the salvation of the town and this means underlining the humanity of cities and enhancing the positive human values of urban life. These are the values that enable human beings to transcend the human condition and to live the true life that is 'hidden with Christ in God'.[14]

The town is a place of human collaboration and initiative, where gifts can be developed for the good of others. It is a place of freedom and individual autonomy. The Church promotes these things by revealing their spiritual dimension. The Church gives to the conspicuously human existence of the town a soul.[15] Human beings are helped to use their freedom responsibly and to see that their ego-centred networks of relationships do not injure the rights and just claims of others. The Christian townsman's motto is the saying of St Paul: 'Whatever you do, do it for the glory of God'.[16]

Urban-dwelling Christians relate their active commitment to Christ to the opportunities, situations and relationships that are characteristic of the town. They also care for the casualties of urban disorientation, deprivation and oppression. Their action is preventive and constructive, not merely remedial or *post factum*. The Christian parish or congregation is truly a house of the Church, a place of silence, welcome, stimulation and renewal, a locus of stability and integration, through which conditions are improved and hearts changed. In the next two chapters we shall consider the ways in which this urban mission of the Church is structured.

References

1 Downes *et al.* 1989. There is a debate among sociologists as to whether declining church attendance indicates a growth of secularism. Religious belief may continue to play an important social role without being centred on active Church commitment. In the author's opinion, however, there are links between the two.

2 Religious affiliation in this survey is based on the claim of individual informants. It is noticeable that where Christians are a dominant element in the population, adherents of traditional religions tend to claim a Christian affiliation. Indigenous Churches tend to have a floating, multiple membership. In fact, a serious analysis of Church affiliation in Nairobi would have to take

account of membership and attendance trends over a period of time.

3 Daystar University College, Nairobi.

4 Kavanaugh 1985; and cf. also note 1 above.

5 Comblin 1968.

6 Ibid.

7 This question also occurs in Chapter 8, where the problem of the integration of youth in the basic Christian communities is discussed.

8 Personal communication from the Reverend J. C. Lemay MAfr, parish priest of Eastleigh.

9 Downes *et al.* 1989, p. 36.

10 Comblin 1968.

11 Mumford 1961.

12 Metz 1980, pp. 32–47.

13 Unpublished autobiography of Francis Caudwell in the author's possession.

14 Colossians 3:3.

15 Comblin 1968.

16 1 Corinthians 10:31.

7

Urban Church structures

'Neighbourliness' in the urban Church

Ujirani mwema is a Swahili phrase meaning 'good neighbourliness' or 'being on good terms with the people next door'. In Dar es Salaam, capital city of Tanzania, it is the name given to the monthly meeting of the Catholic urban deanery. In October 1983 there was a single deanery for the city's Catholic parishes and I was invited to attend and address one of its quarterly meetings at Msimbazi Centre. It was a highly social occasion and certainly lived up to its Swahili ideal of *ujirani mwema*. Msimbazi Centre possesses a spacious compound and attractive buildings in the pavilion style, which, with its open-work walls and high roofs, is well suited to the tropical climate of the East African coast.

The Fathers and Sisters of the parish pastoral teams gathered in a comfortable common room to pray and to discuss the implementation of various diocesan directives. Diocesan financial statements were also read and discussed, after which I was asked to speak about an urban research project on which I was engaged in Tanzania and Kenya. There followed a lively exchange of reactions and experiences. At length the formal part of the meeting came to an end and we adjourned for a buffet supper in an adjoining room. Basically it was a pleasant social occasion at which the representatives of the city parishes could share their problems and concerns in the common interest of the Catholic Church in Dar es Salaam.

Ujirani mwema is an example of how the need for supra-parochial and interparochial structures is already felt in an African city. In this chapter we shall consider the forms such structures take and the functions that are commonly ascribed to them. In particular, we shall see how the deanery, from being a meeting of clergy and religious, can become a zone of pastoral action.

Team ministries

The passive approach of the old-fashioned, all-purpose parish priest is evidently inappropriate in town. Yet, too often, pastors are out of their depths in the urban situation. With no active policy of their own, they try to act alone and to field all the problems that are thrown at them. They improvise from day to day, without a clear plan or purpose. A missionary once wrote to me: 'Our people are lost in the environment of the city: they miss the togetherness and the social relationships of their home parish upcountry'.[1] There is no doubt that migrants find adaptation to town life difficult, but my impression is that the rural missionary is more often 'lost in the environment of the city' than his flock. Of course, if one sits all day in an urban parish office, dealing with an endless stream of callers, coping with correspondence, registers and accounts, one may nourish an illusion of control. However, the problems of those who call are far from representative of the parish as a whole, and the initiative should not lie with them alone. Such behaviour on the part of the pastor is really an abdication of responsibility and leads to pastoral drift. A good parish secretary can handle most of the callers anyway. What the urban parish needs is a parish project or plan and a pastoral team to implement it.

City life today is so complex, so multi-faceted, that team ministries are strictly necessary if evangelization is to be effective. The 1983 Catholic Code of Canon Law foresaw the setting up of a parish pastoral council.[2] This council is conceived as an aid to the parish priest and is composed of lay people, together with those responsible for the pastoral care of the parish. In an urban parish it is necessary that those responsible for pastoral care should form a full-time team which meets more frequently than the pastoral council and independently of it—perhaps on a weekly basis. There may be other bodies such as the parish finance committee,[3] the meeting of community leaders, the Eucharistic ministers, the youth council and so on, but the pastoral team acts as the parish 'steering committee'. It helps the pastor plan parish activities; it analyses problems and situations and it formulates policies. The pastoral team is the 'parish executive', sharing and leading all pastoral activities. In a Catholic town parish, besides the clergy (including permanent deacons, if there are any), there are religious and lay teachers, catechists and community workers, and it is these who form the pastoral team. The team is in close touch with the Eucharistic ministers, the community leaders, the readers, the choir-masters and any other collaborators. In fact, it integrates the whole parish structure.

It is helpful to formulate a parish project or plan. This means stating the underlying goal of evangelization in the parish and working out the steps by which it is to be achieved. It may be useful to plan the various stages of implementation according to a future time-scale. This itself can be an incentive. From week to week the parish team monitors the content of Sunday preaching, of catechetical programmes and community Bible discussions. It organizes seminars, retreats, sessions, days of prayer, services of reconciliation and special liturgical celebrations. Above all, it takes the temperature of the parish through common reflection on its on-going pastoral work.

Urban structures of contact

Traditionally, the Catholic parish priest had an obligation to visit his parishioners. This obligation still appears in the 1983 Code of Canon Law.[4] It is a duty that is increasingly hard to fulfil among the mass populations of Africa's slums and townships, even when there are well-defined numbered plots or houses. Apart from the problems of finding people at home, official visits to individual dwellings may be interpreted as a form of pastoral 'espionage', and even purely social visits can become invidious. On the other hand, visits of the pastoral team to each settlement or neighbourhood are not only pastorally necessary, but deeply appreciated by the committed Christians who live there.

The urban parish, like its rural counterpart, needs a structure of contact. Such a structure takes account, first of all, of the existing micro-environments, the urban geography of association and settlement. Even squatter areas are often divided by government into administrative villages. Where plots are not numbered, toilets, ablution blocks or standpipes may be the reference point. Then there are the so-called 'lines' or compounds of employer-owned housing, as well as the housing estates. It is often practicable to appoint a warden or representative for a street, block or neighbourhood house group.

Rural missionaries, now working in urban parishes, have imported into town the concept of the out-station. The rural out-station is usually the focus for a community of celebration. It is a regular worship centre, and an occasional Mass centre, when a priest is available. In town there is an obvious need to create zones of contact, but it does not follow that such zones should be Mass centres, let alone viable communities. In practice, I have found a widespread confusion of ideas and terminology in the creation of urban contact structures. Various needs have to be identified: the need for centres of worship (and Mass) in areas that are geographically and culturally distinct, if not distant; the need for communication between Christians and their pastors; the need for representation of the different environments in meetings at the parish centre; the need to promote basic ecclesial communities which have a special role and responsibility in the parish. Chapter 8 will be devoted to the problem of building basic communities in the African town. Here let it be said that this process involves much more than the drawing of zones on a parish map or identifying specific micro-environments. By definition, basic ecclesial communities are involved in the pastoral project of the parish, and may even be represented on the pastoral council. Perhaps basic ecclesial communities belong more to the notion of parish as event than to the notion of parish as territory. Whether or not a successful programme of basic community building is being undertaken, I tend to think that the urban parish needs a structure of territorial contact, a hard-and-fast framework of communication and representation within which to operate. Such a zone structure should not be confused with the genuine need for Mass centres. In any case, as far as the Catholic Church is concerned, urban parish churches are usually not far distant from people's homes. However, as the Nairobi survey suggests, the number of worship centres is related to the size of church attendance, and the Catholic Church, in particular, is badly off in this respect.[5]

The two-tier contact structure of Tabora town parish, Tanzania, became a model in East Africa.[6] This is a system of large zones (usually called *kigango* or 'out-station' in Swahili) and a number of sub-divisions or sections (called variously *kikundi*, 'group'; *mtaa*, 'quarter' or 'street'; or more confusingly *jumuiya*, 'community' or *mwungano*, 'union'). Usually, the first tier has a plethora of elected officials: chairman, secretary, treasurer and so on. The second tier normally has one official (called *kiongozi*, 'leader'; or *mlezi*, literally 'tutor' or 'guardian'). It is not a bad thing to create a hierarchy of officials. This is the practice of the indigenous Churches and it gives people a greater sense of participation. However, it must be confessed that it is often an inducement to unwelcome local Church politics. The function of the structure is basically one of communication, letting the pastoral team know of the existence, movements and problems of parishioners, ensuring the attendance of children at catechism, reporting marriage problems, births, deaths, illnesses, social problems, collecting dues, reporting on new projects, distributing relief. In Manzese Catholic Parish, Dar es Salaam, I found in 1982 that there was a regular system of weekly reporting from the zones to the parish centre. In many ways, the structure of contact in an African urban parish is an extension of parish office work.

The structure of contact is intended to cover the whole parish and thus to render the work of the pastoral team a little easier. There is obviously room for discussion about the relation of basic ecclesial communities to the structure of contact. Where they exist, basic communities can perform many of the functions of the contact structure. However, in practice, the number of people involved in the basic communities is relatively small. While they act as a leaven in the entire parish, giving leadership and inspiration to all, the communities usually need to function within a larger contact structure. The pastoral council also needs to reflect this structure, but its functions are even more comprehensive, since it links the pastoral team with all the sectors of interest in the parish: zones, communities, associations, youth movements and so on.

Interparochial urban structures

The limitations of the urban parish require that it be complemented by interparochial structures that can make it more effective. First and foremost among these is the deanery. Deaneries in rural parishes tend to be 'fraternals' rather than places of policy decision and common action. Urban deaneries, on the other hand, operate at close quarters. Their member parishes are not only contiguous, but the parish centres themselves are close to one another. They are much more active in taking common decisions, pooling resources and undertaking common ventures. In this way, they can cope with the transient population that floats among them from centre to centre. In Nairobi City today, for example, the Catholic parishes are grouped into three deaneries, with roughly eight or nine parishes in each. These deaneries are extremely active.

There are many areas for common policy decisions: marriage preparation and campaigns for church marriages, regulations for the administration of the sacraments of initiation, the shape of the catechumenate, the programme for basic community building. One of the parish priests acts as dean and may be given power to dispense from impediments to the sacraments or to confer the sacrament of confirmation in place of the bishop.

90

The deanery is an excellent level at which to pool resources for basic community building, for leadership training, for seminars on Bible study, retreats and so on. Parishes can share the talents of their pastors in youth work or liturgy, for example. In the Eastlands Deanery of Nairobi there are periodic 'Deanery Olympics' which are even reported in the national press, as sporting teams from the Catholic parishes of the deanery compete against each other. Deaneries organize common celebrations in Lent and Advent, or for the celebration of a centenary. Sometimes a deanery newsletter is published. It is not only the pastoral teams from the parishes that meet at deanery level. There are even joint pastoral council meetings. Innumerable problems call for a common solution at deanery level: caring for refugees and abandoned children, administering relief and development aid, or planning ecumenical and inter-faith activities. Promotion of justice and peace, and the social apostolate in general, are always more effective at the interparochial level.

Special urban apostolates will be considered in Chapter 10, but many of these, such as the hospital and prison ministries, are inter-parochial in character. There are also the quasi-parishes and personal parishes mentioned in the previous chapter. Usually, cathedrals and university chaplaincies attract congregations that are drawn from many parts of the city and they may be a favoured place for society weddings and for religious television and radio broadcasts. They often cater for the internationals and the elites of the city, thus performing a service that is beyond the scope of an ordinary parish. Finally, among the interparochial urban structures must be included the general meetings of associations. These can be centralized bodies with branches in the parishes and schools, such as the Legion of Mary, the Young Christian Students, the Pioneers of the Sacred Heart, the Society of St Vincent de Paul in Catholic circles, or the Mothers' Union, the Church Army, the Boys' Brigade among Anglicans. Alternatively, they may be unions of parish-based bodies such as choirs in, let us say, the Catholic Choirs Association. The life of the urban Church is thus articulated through a network of structures that criss-cross the city and that provide for interparochial collaboration in many different ways.

Supra-parochial urban structures

Dioceses are town-based even in the rural areas, but frequently the modern diocese coincides with a gigantic conurbation and becomes virtually a town diocese. Just as the parish is confronted with the problem of population density and population transience, so at the

91

higher level, is the diocese. In the same country of Tanzania, the Catholic archdiocese of Dar es Salaam, which coincides almost entirely with the city itself, has a total population of well over 1½ million, while the Diocese of Njombe has a total population of half a million, and the Diocese of Mbinga barely a quarter of a million. The archbishop of a city like Dar es Salaam, Nairobi, Kampala or Kinshasa cannot hope to pay an annual visit to every parish to administer confirmation. In fact, the sheer size of the city's population makes it impossible for him to carry out personally all his episcopal functions.

One solution is to divide the city itself into suffragan dioceses within a single metropolitan province, as has happened recently in São Paulo, Brazil. Catholic Canon Law foresees the possibility of common pastoral action between suffragan dioceses of a single province, but the Metropolitan is juridically competent only to oversee the faith and discipline of his suffragans, carry out canonical visitations and appoint an administrator where circumstances require it.[7] A city divided into suffragan dioceses is open to the same objections as a city divided into territorial parishes. A much greater degree of co-operation is required. Another solution is for the bishop of the diocese to divide the town/diocese into pastoral areas and assign each area to an auxiliary bishop. This is the solution adopted in Westminster, Southwark and Paris, for example. Auxiliary or area bishops are appointed at the request of the bishop of the diocese. Unless they are named coadjutor, they have no right of succession, and are obliged to function under the diocesan administrator during a vacancy.[8] They 'belong', as it were, to a particular diocesan bishop and cannot undertake any initiatives independently of him. In their more candid moments auxiliary bishops admit to a certain measure of frustration. A pastoral area is not a diocese and there are many things, especially in matters of finance, that an area bishop is not allowed to do. Furthermore, Christians regularly appeal over his head to the diocesan bishop. Perhaps, new canonical legislation is required for multi-diocese cities, to ensure a regular and close co-operation between city suffragans, on the analogy of parishes within the same deanery.

In Catholic Canon Law there are still other options. The bishop of a diocese is empowered to nominate episcopal vicars for particular areas or specific types of activity, and with regard to them they enjoy the same executive power as the bishop himself. However, they are only appointed for a limited period of time.[9] In many ways, therefore, episcopal vicars are even more limited than area bishops. Finally, there are the vicars forane or deans who head the deaneries already discussed above. This office is not attached to any one particular parish, but it carries with it specific responsibilities for promoting common pastoral action among the parishes of the deanery. Their duties include: visitation, overseeing the work and lives of clerics in the deanery, assuring the regularity and authenticity of liturgical functions in the parishes, safeguarding their property, organizing lectures, conferences and theological meetings, providing for the medical treatment of sick clerics, and organizing the funerals of those who die.[10] This admirable list of responsibilities is the foundation for the varied forms of co-operation undertaken by city deaneries. I would submit that the metropolitan of an ecclesiastical province might be accorded analogous responsibilities towards the suffragan bishops of his city. This might go far towards creating a diocesan superstructure for the ever-expanding primate cities of Africa and the rest of the world.

Urban pastorates in rural parishes

In Chapter 3 we considered, among other things, the phenomenon of the mushroom town, the rural township that springs up in a matter of years. Frequently, African town parishes are responsible for a relatively small adjacent rural area. Very different is the situation of the predominantly rural parish in the midst of which one or more townships suddenly make their appearance. I know of no more dramatic example than that of Nzovwe Catholic Parish in Mbeya, Tanzania. When Nzovwe Parish was started in 1951 it had the dual purpose of serving as a chaplaincy to the middle school next door, as well as a rural parish centre. In the early 1950s Nzovwe was a small settlement several miles from Mbeya town. Today, the middle school has become a primary school with an in-service training centre for various categories of teacher attached to it. When I visited Nzovwe a few years ago, two of the parish clergy were involved in religious education on an interparochial basis and a student centre had just been opened. Pastoral activity, however, now had a largely urban character.

Nzovwe was a victim of the remarkable urban growth centred on Mbeya which took place in the 1970s as a result of the building of the Dar es Salaam–Zambia all-weather road and the TAZARA Railway linking Dar es Salaam and Kapiri Mposhi near Lusaka. The railway was laid outside the old boundaries of Mbeya, not far beyond Nzovwe, and a large station and railway complex was created there. The improvement of communications led to rapid industrial development and the creation of extensive new residential areas. Within a decade the town's population quadrupled, from about 25,000 to around 150,000. Nzovwe parish centre has been engulfed by the expanding town of Mbeya, the boundaries of which have pushed far beyond it. The railway workshops employ large numbers of people, as do also a new agricultural implements factory and a soap factory. Most of the workers involved reside in the parish. By the mid-1980s the centre of gravity had shifted from the high ridge on which the old parish centre was situated down to a lower slope called Iyunga, where there is a large secondary school and where the student centre and a new church have been constructed.

The parish of Nzovwe still served fifteen rural out-stations, but two-thirds of the parishioners were by now town dwellers. Six miles away the long-established out-station of Mbalizi has become the site of a meat-packing factory which employs large numbers of workers. Twenty-four miles away, still within the parish boundary, the new town of Songwe is rising, with a textile factory, cement factory and employer-owned housing. A large squatter area has also sprung up beside the factory compounds and not far away is a prison farm. Besides ministering to most of Mbeya's industrial area, the once rural parish of Nzovwe thus serves two further satellite towns, as well as two army barracks, an army prison and numerous schools and colleges. The parish area is now a prey to violent crime, robbery, mugging and alcoholism caused by the rapidly growing affluence of Mbeya.

Nzovwe offers us the example of a rural parish which became predominantly urban. Other parishes, like that of Magu cited in Chapter 3, remain predominantly rural, while coping with a growing town at their centre. Those with pastoral responsibility for such parishes understandably find it difficult to adjust to the changed situation. In some cases, they treat the rising townships as a minority interest in the parish, until they become too important to ignore. The population of African rural areas is expanding, and this growth of townships takes place in a general context of proliferating sub-parishes, out-stations and Mass centres, sometimes as many as fifty or sixty in a parish, served perhaps by only two or three priests. In such a scenario, when townships grow too large to be treated as just another out-station, they are often regarded as an extra burden that hampers work in the rural areas, and pastors cry out for urban specialists to take them off their hands. Before we consider the possible relationship of a new mushroom town to the rest of a rural parish, we must take a look at the types of pastoral structure that are common in rural Africa.

94

Pastoral structures in rural parishes

When there are a large number of villages served by a small number of priests, one method of organizing the apostolate is to group the village out-stations into sub-parishes. In each sub-parish there might be from five to ten out-station chapels or worship-centres. The priest visits the sub-parish centre only for Sunday Mass, and people are expected to travel there when he comes, say once a month. The other out-stations are visited less frequently and Mass is celebrated there on weekdays only. A number of factors are necessary for the successful operation of a sub-parish system. Local Christian leaders need to be active and the programme of visits must be strictly followed. The system works in areas of relatively dense population where there are no formidable geographical obstacles to local travel, such as mountains, lakes or rivers, and where there are good roads and other lines of communication. Even so, there are always those who are unwilling or unable to travel to the sub-parish centre, and Sunday church attendance at the sub-parish is often low. New trends that emphasize self-reliance in the villages do not favour the retention of the sub-parish.

A variant of the sub-parish system is to set up zones with rotating Sunday worship-centres. No one village is designated as a sub-parish centre, but each out-station takes its turn as the venue for the Sunday celebration. Movement between all the villages in the zone is thus encouraged. Needless to say, such a system requires even greater accessibility throughout the zone than the previous one.

A third solution is to conduct successive 'saturation' visits to the zones. This system is suited to areas where villages are far from each other, or there are natural barriers between them. The parish is divided into viable zones which are visited in turn by the pastor for a lengthy period of four to six weeks. During that time Sunday celebrations take place in each village in turn. The next safari will then be to another zone, a month or two later. This method has the disadvantage of longer intervals between the pastoral visits.

Perhaps the problem of coping with large numbers of out-stations in Africa is a peculiarly Catholic one, deriving from the obligations of a sacramental system on the one hand, and the rigorous selection and training of clergy on the other. Other Churches, when they have not been able to create a village clergy, have at any rate created a system of pastoral care that involves considerably less travel. Nevertheless, the success of the Catholic systems depends essentially on the training and co-operation of local lay leaders and helpers. Training and supervision are indispensable for setting up a workable parish structure that can

95

operate independently between the pastoral visits. The ideal is to create a self-servicing pastoral structure into which the priest or pastor can fit, his contribution of sacramental ministry and pastoral supervision being a component in an otherwise on-going lay ministry.

The town as a rural parish resource centre

Urban–rural reinforcement is a feature of modern Africa. Town and country need each other and the two-way flow between them accounts for the phenomenon of urbanization. As we have seen, this interaction may operate to the ultimate disadvantage of the rural areas. Towns can be economically parasitic on the countryside, but they may also generate income for rural communities. One of the Church's social tasks is to ensure that there is a better balance between urban giving and urban taking, more service and less domination by the town. Ideally, the rural township is a resource centre for the agricultural areas. It shares ideas, plans and policies. It distributes commodities and creates job opportunities. The size of population and pluralism of experience in the town generate freedom, autonomy, choice and creativity. The town is a place of education and a favoured venue for the educated. It is the mission of the Church to place all these positive advantages at the service of Christ and of the whole community, rural as well as urban.

There is a sense in which a rural parish also needs a town. The town is, materially speaking, a resource centre for commodities, fuel and expertise. Even the small town is able to service vehicles and machines. It is better stocked, better equipped, than the villages. But why should the town be a material resource centre only? Why should it not also be a spiritual resource centre? The town is already a place of rest for returning pastors, a place for re-equipping the next safari to the out-stations. It is also a place of training and formation and a place of administration, organization and distribution. Usually, the parish centre and parish office are situated in or near the rural town. Where this was not the case, it has been felt necessary to move them there. Sometimes, too, there is a parish store or co-operative shop to help parishioners obtain commodities at reasonable prices. The parish pastoral council meets at the parish centre, so do the catechists and community leaders for retreats and training sessions.

In view of these realities, it would be a good idea to mobilize the resources of the town for the good of the parish as a whole and make it a place of pastoral and spiritual service to the surrounding area. Furthermore, such a project might be integrated into a programme of urban spiritual awakening also. Educated and committed Christian townsmen could be recruited for the formation of rural leaders, for the improvement of Christian family life and for catechetical and liturgical creativity. Town-based pastoral teams might be set up to visit the villages, so that not only the priest is on safari. All this would provide a religious counterpart for the secular role of townsmen. Rural Christians could also offer a witness to townsfolk through these means. If neighbourliness can be shown between villages in a zone, it is surely possible to do the same between villages and the rural town.

At the same time, Christian townsmen could be helped to reflect on the socio-economic relationship between town and countryside, and between rural towns and the larger towns. They could be helped to become more aware of the long-term effects of urbanization, its advantages and disadvantages, and try to confront the issues of social justice that are involved. Rural community leaders who move to town should be encouraged to set up urban basic communities.

Somehow the rural town has to be viewed as something other than an extra pastoral burden, something more than an overgrown out-station. Towns are an integral part of the socio-economic system. Their existence has to be confronted realistically by the Church. Rather than an extra pastoral burden, they should be viewed as an extra pastoral resource. Greater attention paid to the rural town need not be at the expense of the surrounding rural areas. Having examined urban ecclesial structures and the role of towns in rural parishes, we go on to consider in the next chapter the creation of basic ecclesial communities in towns and cities.

References

1 Shorter 1983a, p. 8.
2 Canon 536.
3 Canon 537.
4 Canon 529.
5 Downes *et al.* 1989, p. 34.
6 This model was introduced by the late Father Jan Brouwer MAfr, when he was parish priest of Tabora in the 1970s and 1980s.
7 Canons 431–434; 435–436.
8 Canons 403–411.
9 Canons 476–481.
10 Canons 553–554.

8

Basic Christian communities in the African town

Community meeting in Pangani

People were already assembling when I arrived for the Pangani basic Christian community meeting one Tuesday evening in 1984. Pangani is a run-down low-income estate in Nairobi City's Eastlands. The venue for the meeting was a somewhat dingy compound behind a one-storey dwelling house near the main road. On two sides of the enclosed space were rooms for renting and on the third an ablution block. A single electric light bulb yielded a fitful glimmer as the sun sank behind the roof. Stoves glowed outside several doorways. Radios played African pop music and a mixture of cooking smells and less inviting odours mingled in the evening air. The small Christian community of the neighbourhood held its weekly meeting here, but it was apparent that not all the residents would be attending, and that life would go on regardless. It was a very African situation, this tolerance towards a Christian invasion of daily life.

It took about half an hour for the community members to assemble, and several latecomers slipped in after the meeting had begun. Some twenty people attended in all. A tall, unkempt young man, who was the community leader, invited us to sing an opening hymn. The Swahili words rose and fell on the evening air, drowning out the domestic sounds around us:

> I raise my heart to you, Father;
> Guard me from evil; you are my only hope.

Show me your ways, teach me your truth;
May your wisdom guide me; you are my only hope.

I glanced round the assembled group in the fading light. Most of the members were women clad in bright cotton dresses and head-scarves, but there were a fair number of men in jeans and jackets or pullovers. There were a few small children and a sprinkling of teen-agers. Most were clutching the small blue hymnbook-cum-prayer-book that was popular in the parish. At the leader's suggestion, some prayers were cited from the book. Then one of the women read the Gospel of the following Sunday from a small Swahili New Testament. It was about the calling of the first apostles. A period of silence followed the reading and I found it difficult to concentrate amid the noises of the adjacent slum. Then the leader invited us to share our reactions to the reading. How was it that the apostles felt compelled to follow the call of Jesus? What had they left behind? What did it mean to be fishers of men? A discussion followed which gradually gathered momentum. The men spoke first, but the women soon joined in, testifying to the importance of the Gospel in their lives. Jesus had called them through this small Christian community and they were working with him to change people's hearts and to show them his love.

By now it was almost completely dark. The only points of light were the distant light bulb and the leader's flashlight poised over his book. It was time for announcements. There were some communications from the parish priest and reports from a couple of meetings at parish level. Then members were asked to report on their work for the community. Visits to sick people were described and help given to the destitute of the area. The question of how the community could assist a certain refugee was also discussed and there was a lively exchange about incidents of police harassment in the neighbourhood. There was also a report from a community member who had attended a basic community meeting in the neighbouring squatter area. 'They are Christians the same as we are', she said simply. After this, the leader commenced the bidding-prayers. There were a great many petitions, some of them quite lengthy, and punctuated again and again with the invocation *Ee Baba*, 'O Father'. The Lord's Prayer was then recited by all, and the meeting ended with the singing of 'When we love one another, God is in our midst'. Some of the group stayed to talk, but most dispersed in the dark to their homes.

Basic communities differ from one neighbourhood to another. Their character and central concerns vary; so, too, does the format of their meetings. Yet I believe that this particular community was fairly typical of the movement that has swept through the Church in eastern Africa since the 1970s. In this chapter we examine the functioning of such communities in the urban situation. In my opinion, they are the most important initiative of the urban Church in Africa today.

Community as a traditional rural value

President Kenneth Kaunda of Zambia described the traditional African community as 'mutual, accepting and inclusive'.[1] Its mutuality consisted in the reciprocal relations of its members. It accepted people as they were, with their weaknesses and their disabilities. It was so inclusive that even death was not a barrier to continued membership. Kaunda goes so far as to declare that the sense of community is built into the psychology of the African. Be that as it may, community is certainly a social undertaking that is, by definition, conscious and willed. To begin with, it is based on a common field of experience from which arise shared understandings and judgements, but it is only when there are common commitments that community can really be said to come into existence.

Community cannot survive without the kind of mutual trust and readiness to listen that encourages self-revelation. Community also presupposes a basic equality and a basic claim to mutual assistance. On the other hand, it demands mutual respect and recognition of personal freedom. In a close-knit community individuals need their own psychological elbow-room. That, for instance, is why villagers in rural Africa are so punctilious about greetings and formal modes of address. As we saw in Chapter 2, village communities in Africa are focused on a locality, a common occupation and life-style. These constitute the common experiential field that is the basis for psychological proximity and social reciprocity. The traditional African community is 'basic' in the sense that it is life-embracing, a vehicle for social integration at the wider level.[2] In Latin America, however, a community is described as 'basic' when it identifies with the lowest social strata, the poor and the oppressed.

There is no doubt that traditional community in Africa is affected adversely by social change and by what we have called 'peri-urbanization' in the wide sense. Increased population migration and job mobility have enlarged the scale of relationships. The family community is no longer effective, and village neighbourhood communities are increasingly transient and differentiated, instead of being stable and homogeneous. Social stratification is also undermining rural community through development programmes and new administrative structures. The spread of an urban consciousness, with its emphasis on network and work focus, also plays its part in the process.

The revival of community within the Christian Church is not unrelated to this sad history; in fact, Christian communities, particularly those of the indigenous religious movements, very often function as adaptive mechanisms, substituting for family and village.[3] The Church in Africa has been rurally oriented, but not necessarily community oriented. Out-station centres were set up by mission-related Churches for the convenience of the pastor, rather than that of the community.[4] Monolithic structures, such as dioceses and parishes, were created and defined in terms of large-scale territory, rather than small-scale settlement. The individual-in-the-crowd was preferred to the human-in-community. Churches were sacralized, clerical, incapsulated. Against this tradition, the widespread adoption of small Christian communities as a pastoral priority entailed a measure of decentralization and declericalization. Henceforward, local initiatives would be welcome, and people would pray, celebrate and live the Gospel in the places where they lived and worked. In Africa, basic community building by the Churches was originally a rural enterprise. As we saw in Chapter 2, urban social organization is largely antagonistic to traditional forms of community, and that is why there is a lurking suspicion that basic communities, being originally a rural experiment, may be inappropriate in towns.

Basic community as a Christian concept

Basic ecclesial communities began as a reaction to the concept of the Church as a vast, impersonal organization controlled by the hierarchy, an organization in which the laity had only 'to pray, pay and obey'. In many ways, they are a renaissance of the Church.[5] Although they are partly born out of a crisis in Christian ministry—the lack of ordained ministers—they are not an alternative to the Church's hierarchical structure, as some uninformed people suppose. On the contrary, the development of basic ecclesial communities within Church structures attributes new or additional functions to the hierarchy and helps to renew and reorientate the Church's organization. Basic ecclesial communities are not the whole Church, but they are 'Church' (ecclesial) in a real sense, at the level of the people's concrete life. If the family can be called the 'domestic Church' because it proclaims, celebrates and lives the Gospel of Christ, then basic communities are

101

called 'ecclesial' because they, too, are 'beneficiaries' and 'proclaimers' of the Gospel and 'cause the Church to grow'.[6]

Basic ecclesial communities started in Brazil and Panama in the 1950s, as a creative pastoral effort of the laity, supported by the Catholic bishops. In the 1960s and 1970s they sprang up in many Latin American countries: Chile, Peru, Paraguay, El Salvador and Nicaragua. In these countries they represent the 'grass-roots' of the Church, the landless *campesino* and, increasingly, the squatter in the urban *barrio* or *favela*. In fact, it is estimated that now basic ecclesial communities are more numerous in the town than in the village. It seems that in Latin America, at any rate, basic ecclesial communities are as much at home in the urban areas as in the rural areas. From Latin America basic community building has spread to other parts of the Hispanic world, notably the Philippines.

Basic ecclesial communities have been associated with Liberation Theology, with the preferential option for the poor, and with Paulo Freire's programme of conscientization through which the poor come to understand their unjust socio-economic situation and discover their power to change it. They reflect a new, evangelical, prophetic way of understanding social realities, and they represent a trend away from a paternalistic Church and towards a Church of full, lay participation. At Medellín in 1968 and at Puebla in 1979, the Latin American bishops gave basic ecclesial communities their full support.

The Catholic bishops of Eastern Africa (AMECEA) adopted the building of 'small Christian communities' as a pastoral priority in 1973, partly in response to the Latin American experience and partly as a follow-up to the Nairobi Catechetical Congress of that year, which adopted the slogan 'Towards Adult Christian Community'. Successive plenary study sessions in 1976 and 1979 reiterated the AMECEA pastoral policy, as did SECAM, the continental Catholic episcopal association, at its 1984 Kinshasa meeting. The stated purpose of the policy was threefold: to ensure that people could practise their Christian faith in the places where they work and live, to bring about a greater lay participation, and to provoke a more authentic localization (inculturation). Not only was there to be a decentralization to the out-station, but a measure of decentralization to neighbourhood household groups called 'small Christian communities' or, in Swahili, *jumuiya ndogo ndogo*.

The subsequent history of the implementation of this policy in Africa clearly showed that one cannot carry out a transition from a paternalistic Church *for* the people to a mature Church *of* the people by simply ordering it from above. This merely emphasizes the

102

paternalism and makes the small Christian communities an extension of existing hierarchical structures. Events showed that, instead of a master-plan created in the bishop's office, the experiment had to be started from below, in suitable environments and with suitable leadership. Where this happened, the experiment was successful and the bishops' expectations were justified. It must also be admitted that joining a small Christian community is not the only way of practising the Christian commandment of universal love; there will always be some people for whom the network, rather than the group, will be the favoured medium of Christian charity.

Community as an urban reality in Africa

Earlier, in Chapter 2, it was pointed out that community is essentially a rural form of social life, and that—apart from certain micro-environments, such as the urban squatter villages—there is little social cohesion of a community type in the city. Nevertheless, experience shows that it is not impossible to set up small Christian communities in urban parishes, as long as one recognizes that they will be different from their rural counterparts. Firstly, as we have already seen, although geography should be taken broadly into account, one must not confuse small Christian communities with contact zones or report groups in the parish contact structure. Communities do not appear where we want them simply because we command them to appear there, least of all in a hostile urban environment. The experience of pastors in urban parishes has demonstrated that they can only be formed in towns around committed emergent leaders.[7] Leaders must be sought and trained, and then sent back to their residential areas to begin forming a small Christian community. Seminars for training community leaders are therefore indispensable for urban community building.

To be viable in town, basic communities must be considerably larger than their rural counterparts. They also tend to be unstructured and unwieldy.[8] Membership tends to fluctuate more than in the rural areas and meetings are bigger. Membership is ultimately undefined and shades off into a series of networks at the edges. The fission, fusion and fade-out of small Christian communities is more rapid in the town. The Pangani community, for example, which was cited at the beginning of this chapter, has had several vicissitudes. At the height of its expansion, it divided into two, and a sub-group started an independent meeting across the road. Later, the two communities coalesced again when the new group dwindled. Increased numbers often force a community into fission, just as reduced numbers force communities to fuse; but frequently, at the outset, people are reluctant to make the change, and a dramatic event is necessary to make them aware of the need. In a community in another part of Nairobi Archdiocese, the meetings were held in a large bed-sitting-room, and the need to divide was only recognized when a bed collapsed under the weight of the half-dozen persons sitting on it! The universal temptation is to think of basic communities as static and unchanging, when in actual fact they are living social realities that are born, grow, die and are born again.

Servicing urban basic communities

In view of what has been said, it is clear that urban basic communities probably require more care, attention and maintenance than rural basic communities. However, they should not depend wholly on the visits of a priest or member of the pastoral team in order to function properly, to solve their problems, or to replace leaders. Urban parishes have come to rely on regular meetings of all the basic community leaders, and these constitute their own service team. Besides the functioning of this service team, there should also be mutual visits and joint activities between the various basic communities. This is easier to achieve in an urban parish than in a rural one, since distance is less of a problem. However, there are other barriers than those of distance—the barriers between different micro-environments and subcultures, for example. Quite often, Christians in a housing estate are suspicious of those who live in an adjacent squatter area. They assume, perhaps understandably, that squatters are the cause of robbery, mugging and other criminal activities, and they are not anxious to invite them into their homes or compounds for a Christian community meeting. Yet the only way to remove prejudice is by associating with squatters and airing their suspicions. The networking of basic communities is useful everywhere; in the town it is indispensable, in view of population transience and the high concentration of Christians in the parish.

When urban people move house, they sometimes choose to remain with their previous basic community, if it is not out of reach. If there is no community in their new neighbourhood, they may be instrumental in setting one up. Experience shows that when Christians from squatter or slum areas, where conditions favour the creation of basic communities, move to higher-income areas that are inherently less favourable to community, such 'spiralists' have more success in community building than the pastoral team. As convinced and experienced community members, they stand a better chance of spreading the basic community concept than the pastors themselves.

Urban basic communities contribute to the life of the parish as a whole. As we already suggested in Chapter 7, they may send representatives to the parish pastoral council, but they should have a free, floating relationship with parish structures, since freedom is an essential characteristic of community itself. The basic communities are 'ecclesial', that is, a way of being Church, but there are other ways of being Church. It may happen that in an urban parish where 6,000 people attend the Sunday worship-centres, less than 1,000 belong to the small Christian communities. Obliging people as a matter of policy to report to the local basic community when they want their baby baptized, their child confirmed or their marriage blessed, may ultimately be counter-productive. Educated and affluent people find it difficult to submit to the scrutiny of uneducated, low-class community leaders; and the latter may find it equally difficult to overcome their antipathy towards the affluent. The preferential option for the poor undoubtedly demands co-operation across barriers of economic class and schooling, but such co-operation may only be the outcome of a lengthy process of religious re-education. It is important to have other solutions to hand for those who, for one reason or another, find it difficult to join a basic community, even if the communities normally collaborate with the pastoral team in vetting candidates for the sacraments.

Small Christian communities are very different in purpose from the old parish associations that are adjuncts of the parish structure, rather than expressions of particular real-life situations. Nevertheless, it is often the case that the community leaders are members of the associations and that the latter offer the communities a spirituality that is valuable for their collective prayer, Bible enquiry and apostolic action. There are also other relatively new movements in the Church, which may even be house-based like the basic communities. Such are charismatic groups, prayer-groups, Gospel-enquiry groups, ecumenical discussion groups, poverty-action groups, justice and peace groups and so on. In themselves, these are not basic ecclesial communities, although it may be possible to convert them into such. In 1988–89 a team of lay missionaries, working in a Nairobi Catholic parish, converted fifteen prayer-groups into small Christian communities, helping them acquire a pastoral and a social justice dimension. It may not, however, be possible or desirable to convert such groups into basic communities, and none of these movements, even those that cater for

Christians of a particular ethnic group or economic class, need be in competition with the communities. All these organizations have their place in the urban parish and mutually invigorate one another.

The tasks of urban basic communities

The main task of the basic ecclesial community in the city is that of unifying and intensifying Christian living, by focusing on life and work contexts, by crossing the inner frontiers of the parish, and countering all forms of pluralism—ethnic, economic, and educational. The basic communities make use of everyone's gifts in the effort to live the Christian faith in a particular environment or life-situation. The tasks of these communities can be roughly divided into pastoral tasks and tasks of witness. Pastoral tasks include: marriage preparation; marriage counselling and support of married couples; care for, prayer with, the sick and disabled; preparation of children for the sacraments of initiation; help in the running of the adult catechumenate; parent and godparent formation; shared prayer and devotions; contributing to the liturgical life of the parish; home visiting; attending and giving retreats and seminars; and being a Eucharistic community in the wide sense. The last means that the basic community is not the regular place of Eucharistic celebration, but that it is the life-context in which the Eucharist is anticipated and afterwards lived.

The urban situation lends itself to the performance of many of these pastoral tasks. Home visiting is more easily conducted by members of a town-based local community. Holding of prayer services, e.g. the Catholic Stations of the Cross, in successive dwellings can be readily organized. Community contributions to parish liturgical and catechetical events can be arranged with comparative ease. In many urban parishes in Africa, on the great festival days, the community leaders join the procession of clergy and choristers, carrying the crosses or placards that bear the name of their communities. In this way, the basic communities are accorded recognition by the whole parish.

The witnessing tasks of the basic communities include: relating the Bible to life; working for justice and peace; running co-operative shops; caring for refugees; distributing poor relief; managing kindergartens; organizing vigilante groups; teaching health care and getting the sick to hospital; conducting literacy classes and teaching in basic education units; encouraging apprentice training; making use of group media. It requires a constant effort to ensure that basic ecclesial communities 'step out of the sacristy and into the street', by confronting the justice issues of everyday life. Group media are useful for expressing the communities' identity and for communicating within the communities' network. Popular forms of group media in Africa include: choirs, newsletters, drama, poetry writing and recitation. Small Christian communities have their own choirs and drama groups that perform at the parish centre, and both drama and song play an important role in both worship and Bible study. It is not far-fetched to argue that basic communities are laboratories of inculturation in Africa.[9]

Basic community in the suburbs

Establishing neighbourhood house groups in the suburbs is more difficult than setting up basic communities in the squatter villages and low-income areas of the city. We have already seen the reason for this.[10] Suburban dwellers insulate themselves against the rest of the city by creating their own home environment, their own garden exclusion-zone. For many, their home is little more than a dormitory to which they return after a day at the office, ready to relax briefly with their families in front of the television. Otherwise, they spend their evenings in the company of their peers at the many bars, restaurants and places of night entertainment that the city provides. The creation of local neighbourhood groups in such circumstances is far from easy.

Nevertheless, community-building is the natural accompaniment of evangelization, and the Gospel must be brought to bear on suburban life contexts and work interests. I believe it is possible to create issue-centred or even Christian professional groups of various kinds, dealing with such matters as: justice and peace, the social apostolate, ecumenism, consumer monitoring, conservation of the environment, and so forth. Groups of Christian professionals already exist in African cities; and some are highly structured and active. However, they have to be ecclesial or 'Church'. This means that they must operate within Church structures and adopt Christian pastoral and witnessing roles, as well as enjoy their own life of prayer nourished by Bible reading and discussion.

Suburban basic communities may also stem from renewal movements such as Parish Renewal, the Better World Movement, the Focolare movement and other bodies. Some of these might also develop into basic ecclesial communities with their own relationship of prayer to life. The most important factor, however, to be borne in mind when promoting community-building in the suburbs is, as was suggested in Chapter 6, to link suburban groupings in some way to those of the poorer majority in the city, and to enable the affluent to help remove urban structures of injustice.

Community and anti-structure

The house-church movement has grown up in Britain and America among people who, for one reason or another, resist the imposition of larger ecclesial structures.[11] It is a movement with a long history going back to early Methodism in the eighteenth century, and perhaps even to the groups of Illuminati in the Middle Ages, the Waldensians, Cathars and Albigensians. It seems to belong to a Reformation tradition in which ecclesial polity is relativized, and which gives rise to proliferating families of tiny house churches, such as the Harvestine, Chard and Fullness Churches in Britain, or the Women Churches and underground groups in America. Such a trend would not be a normal development in many of the mission-related Churches in Africa, which adhere to stronger notions of a more visible communion among local groupings, but it seems to be a characteristic of some indigenous religious movements.

There is always a healthy tendency in community towards anti-structure. This was an axiom of the late Victor Turner in his brilliant anthropological study of the sense of community.[12] Communities resist the imposition of structures and the tendency towards institutionaliz-ation, in order to serve better the values of freedom and equality. They cannot surrender these principles and become the blind instruments of hierarchy, status and structure. If they were to do so, they would cease to be communities. On the other hand, if Christian communities wish to be truly ecclesial, they must be in communion with one another, and that means operating within the structures of ecclesial communion. This is the paradox of the basic ecclesial community with which Pope Paul VI tried to come to grips in *Evangelii Nuntiandi*.[13] It is a paradox that is acutely felt in urban situations, for, while inter-community networking is physically easier in town, community autonomy and factionalism are constant temptations. These temp-tations partly arise from the interaction and overlap of many different kinds of religious community in the African city: parishes, out-stations, worship-centres, small communities and other groupings in the poly-ethnic mission-related Churches, on the one hand, and indigenous Church movements, healing communities and pentecostal groups, many of which have an ethnic bias, on the other. Ministering to urban basic communities in mission-related or mainline Churches requires considerable social and psychological skill, besides the necessary faith and stamina, if the delicate balance between ecclesial community and ecclesial communion is to be maintained. However, in the final analysis, the successful evangelization of the city depends on maintaining that tension. The structure of territory and hierarchy has to be complemented by the anti-structure of community, if the Gospel is to be lived.

Nothing has been said in this chapter about the particular problems of youth participating in the life of basic ecclesial communities in the African town. This aspect of the question is reserved for the following chapter, which deals extensively with the problems of urban youth and their pastoral care. The youth constitute the largest element in the age-structure of African towns, and questions that affect them have a bearing on every aspect of the Church's urban mission. After examining the question of urban youth, other special apostolates in the city will be examined in Chapter 10. Among these, the ecumenical movement is given pride of place, because the town is everywhere—and not least in Africa—a place of privileged encounter between Churches and religious faiths.

References

1 Kaunda and Morris 1966.

2 Perrin-Jassy 1973 gives this meaning to 'basic community' in Africa.

3 This is a major thesis of Perrin-Jassy 1973.

4 Kalilombe 1984.

5 Cf. Boff 1986.

6 Paul VI, *Evangelii Nuntiandi*, 58, 71.

7 Cf. Edele 1977; Father Andreas Edele's experience was in two parishes of Lusaka, Zambia.

8 For this reason, in Nairobi's Eastleigh Catholic Parish the small Christian communities are not called *jumuiya ndogo ndogo*, 'small communities', but *mwungano*, 'reunion'.

9 Cf. Shorter 1988, pp. 267–70.

10 Cf. Chapter 4.

11 Clark 1984, pp. 87–9.

12 Turner 1969.

13 *Evangelii Nuntiandi*, 58.

9

The pastoral care of urban youth

Why did Kalulu die?[1]

One day in March 1985 a speeding taxi ran over and killed a small eight-year-old boy on a busy road near East Africa's infamous shanty-town, Mathare Valley. The accident happened at around nine o'clock at night. There are many such accidents in the area, usually involving children and old people. Several times a year the priests of the nearby Catholic parish baptize a dying child by the roadside or absolve an elderly person knocked down by a hit-and-run car or bus. Driving is erratic in the city and accidents are far too numerous. In fact, a few days before the boy's death, I myself had given conditional absolution to a man lying in the road in a pool of blood. There was no sign of police or ambulance, and I took the man to hospital in my own car. But what was a small boy of eight doing on these dangerous roads at night?

To start with, Kalulu was a nickname. Few people knew the boy's real name. His mother was not worried when Kalulu failed to come home that night. He often slept away from home, as did his elder brother. Kalulu was what people called a *chokora*, a street scavenger, one of the thousands of such children who roam the streets day and night, scavenging for food in dustbins and rubbish dumps. Sometimes they beg food from street vendors, maize-roasters and vegetable sellers. Sometimes the youngsters hang around the bars and night-clubs and are given alcohol and cigarettes. A practice that many have developed is to dip rags into the petrol tanks of cars and sniff petrol in order to get high and forget their hunger and cold. At night

110

they sleep in a huddle under newspapers or cardboard in the markets or public toilets. It is difficult to wean them from the freedom of the streets.

In spite of his dirty, ragged appearance, Kalulu was a lovable little boy, always smiling and full of pranks. He loved to march solemnly up to the altar in church and sit down in the front row. When the time came for the kiss of peace, he would thrust his grubby little hand into the hands of all around him, enjoying the hesitation and disdain on their faces. At other times, he would go to the primary school and make funny faces at the pupils through the windows, until the teacher chased him away. He begged from everybody. He was everyone's child. In my earlier, idealistic days I tried to help Kalulu by giving him some new clothes that I had received for poor children. The parish sacristan took Kalulu, his brother and another small friend and gave them a bath. After they had all been scrubbed, the sacristan told me that the bath water looked like coffee. The youngsters enjoyed their first contact with soap and donned the new clothes with glee. For half a day they swaggered around self-consciously. Next day they appeared again in dirty rags as before, having sold the clothes I gave them. I learned that it was more sensible for me to fill my car up with street kids and drive them round to a kiosk for a plate of food. It is no use giving new clothes to them unless it is part of a wider strategy of rehabilitation.

Kalulu was not at home on the fatal night, because of the poverty of his mother. Like many unmarried mothers in the shanty-town, she had 'boyfriends' who helped her to pay the rent and survive. This casual prostitution meant that the children were not wanted at home. Moreover, the woman was constantly being evicted for failure to pay her rent. She tried her hand at brewing illicit liquor, but did not have the financial outlay required for the bribes needed to escape police harassment. And so she moved around, hoping to attract new 'boyfriends'. For Kalulu, home did not really exist.

Kalulu was given a big funeral. One of the priests paid for the coffin, and as many street kids as possible were rounded up to attend. Press photographers and journalists had also been invited in order to report on the event and give publicity to the social problems underlying little Kalulu's death. Some parishioners raised their eyebrows at the funeral honours paid to a *chokora*, but, besides paying respect to a lovable human being made in God's image and redeemed by him, it was an occasion to cause people to ponder the factors that lie behind the deaths of children like Kalulu. In this chapter, we shall attempt

111

to examine the whole problem of the pastoral care of children and young people in the African city.

Africa's street children

Thousands of undernourished children roam the streets of African towns and cities. They survive by means of theft and expediency. Without affection, education and the security of family life, they are abused and maltreated by adults whom they regard as enemies. What kind of adults are they themselves likely to become? Up to 70 per cent of Africa's town dwellers are 'youth': children, teenagers and young adults under thirty. Children of between five and fifteen years of age constitute perhaps a third of urban youth in Africa, and many of these are on the streets.[2] Our instinctive feeling is that children should have a loving home and family and that they should enjoy the benefits of education in a school. Their growing bodies are in need of proper nourishment and health care. As far as society is concerned, children have a right to all these things. Older, non-urbanized Africans, with their traditions of family community and their strong desire to generate human life, are often shocked, and even disbelieving, when told about street children in African towns. They cannot imagine a situation in which children are separated from the parental family. Yet, 'un-African' as it seems, the facts are there for all to see. It goes without saying that decent people frown on prostitution, thieving and drug-taking, yet, from the point of view of the street children themselves, these are survival strategies. Girls are seldom prostitutes from choice. They may be using their only available asset, the ability to exploit the sexual proclivities of men. They are subjected to pressures that are seldom considered by those who condemn prostitution out of hand. The unlawfulness of theft is attenuated when the child thief is continually denied the right to food, clothing and life itself. The majority of street children take drugs to accomplish acts that go against their nature, or to overcome fear or misery. African street children are out of school because the education system, in one way or another, excludes them. Those who have experienced African street children at first hand (Andrew Hake, Arnold Grol, and Fabio Dallape, for example) were surprised to find that, although they are understandably ill at ease with school discipline, they are nonetheless avid for education.

The rehabilitation of street children by the Church, or by any social agency, requires that the values of the children themselves be taken into account. Rehabilitation must be built on these values.

African street children want to learn; they know how to survive and how to organize themselves. They possess a high degree of solidarity among themselves. Also, they are creative and ready for any profitable work. The lack of normal family life means that street children must reinvent the family. They do this through their gang life. The street gangs of urban Africa are a form of socialization by peers and they have been extensively described. They include the Parking Boys of Nairobi, the cigarette-vending Mishanga Boys of Lusaka, the Market Boys of Kampala, the Red Xhosa and Soweto Children of urban South Africa, and the Indoubils of Kinshasa.[3] A sketch of an African street gang might look something like the following.

Mwaura is the leader of a gang in a Nairobi squatter settlement. He is sixteen years old and his gang is called 'Base', because the broken-down abandoned shanty where they sleep is not far from an airforce base. The gang also has its own private 'language', a variant of Sheng, the mixture of Swahili, English and Kikuyu that is spoken in the Nairobi slums. Mwaura's gang is composed of seven members, two of whom are only eleven or twelve years old. These are in the service of the five older boys who are teenagers. Mwaura is a natural leader and the shanty belongs to him. The other boys ask his permission for anything they do. The gang members care for one another, and the weaker ones are protected by the stronger, provided they accept their authority. The gang is run like a business company, with its own rules and its own discipline. Each member is used according to his talents in order to make money. Two act as parking-boys, showing motorists where to park downtown, and helping to carry shopping back to the parked cars. One is looking after a herd of goats for someone in the shanty-town, guiding them to the barely available grazing. Two others are scavenging for saleable items in the refuse heaps, while another is an 'artful dodger', picking pockets, stealing bags, and faking accidents at traffic crossings so as to be paid on-the-spot 'hush money' by motorists. Finally, Mwaura himself is an apprentice mechanic at a garage. Everyone in the gang has to be productive. Some receive more of the day's takings than others, in accordance with the gang's hierarchy. Mwaura himself receives the most, and this helps to pay for his garage training. At the end of a good day, the gang sometimes shares its earnings with friends or holds a party. Mwaura takes on the role of a parent, warning the younger boys against excessive drug-taking or drinking of alcohol, taking them to a dispensary when they are sick, or going for help when they are arrested by the police.

Church-founded organizations try to help African street children

113

in accordance with the Church's perceived urban mission of building on positive human values. The restoration of family life and the return to rural communities of origin are laudable objectives, but they can seldom be realized. Street children are separated from their families by grave obstacles and problems which have to be resolved before reunification can take place.[4] The children may have been maltreated or neglected. They may feel ashamed of their parents, particularly their mother, if she is a prostitute. The parents may not be capable, for one reason or another, of fulfilling their parental role, and considerable behavioural change may be demanded of them before the children can stay with them. Attempts by the Churches and the courts to return the children to rural homes nearly always fail. Even less likely to succeed are the brutal methods occasionally employed by the police of rounding up street children, giving them a beating at the police station, and taking them home in lorries. In most cases, the children are back in town again before the police who took them away!

In any case, many of the children were born in town; their fathers are unknown and there are no paternal relatives to accept responsibility for them. A number of children are also effectively abandoned by their mothers. For these, the best solution is to develop the gang principle in a wholesome manner by providing foster homes and artificial families. In some cases, it has been possible to offer agricultural training to street children, with the prospect of a career in the rural areas.[5] However, it is unrealistic to imagine that the flow of urban migrants can somehow be reversed. For most of the street children, basic education must be given in the urban areas themselves. In Nairobi, the Undugu Basic Education Units were recognized by the Ministry of Education. They allow the street children to combine class attendance with their daily 'business' activities — literacy, numeracy and a knowledge of current affairs being the main goals of the system. After this, the way is open for the youngsters to attend a trade school or 'village polytechnic'.

Another problem that concerns the children in towns is child abuse.[6] In the rural areas it is normal for children to work in the home or in the fields and pastures, but in the urban areas, child labour is no longer confined to family or domestic chores. Children become a business asset or an economic resource. They keep shop, or act as truckers, porters or touts. When families are very poor, they hire out their children as labour to earn money. This produces a system akin to slavery in which children become commodities that are bought and sold. The child becomes a housemaid, kitchen boy, messenger or cleaner, and the security of home and family is exchanged for the household of an employer concerned with maximizing profits, rather than child-rearing. In such employment, children are frequently maltreated or even sexually exploited.

Many small children are obliged to accompany their mothers to prison when they are convicted of crime, and this experience may leave lifelong mental and moral scars. Children who remain outside prison during their mother's sentence are frequently at the mercy of neighbours who exploit them or maltreat them. Yet another category of disadvantaged urban children are those who have experienced war situations and who, in some cases, have been child soldiers. Such youngsters have to be rehabilitated and educated for non-violence, justice and peace.[7]

Orientation and mentality of urban youth

Teenagers and young adults between the ages of fifteen and thirty make up the bulk of Africa's urban youth and in most cases constitute around 50 per cent of the town population. When Africans speak about 'youth',[8] they mean those who belong to this broad age category, and the term even includes young married people. Africans tend to preserve a great deal of youthful vitality, enthusiasm and even appearance up to mid-life. This does not necessarily imply a lack of maturity, though a certain degree of prolonged juvenile immaturity and irresponsibility may be encouraged by starting school late in life, by the prolongation of schooling, and by the experience of parental authoritarianism. Urban youth in Africa, however, enjoys a greater measure of freedom and autonomy than its rural counterpart, and this is undoubtedly part of the town's attraction. African youth is urban-oriented to a massive degree and the youth populations of African cities and towns are well above the national average, even though family life is unstable in the urban areas and many young children of urban parents are still brought up in the rural homelands.[9] In fact, the average age of the adult populations of African cities and towns is considerably lower than in the rural areas, owing to the high proportion of youth among the urban migrants.

Towns are favoured sites for secondary schools, universities and colleges; and students are an important, though numerically small, element among the urban youth. Much more numerous are the school-leavers who flock to town, asserting independence from their families and either seeking or creating employment for themselves. Urban life exercises a powerful attraction for young people. Part of

115

this attraction lies in the urban leisure industries that are specifically geared to the youth. Sport, music, dancing, film shows and bars draw them to the urban areas. Bars and discos bear names that echo the leisure-ethic: *Furahisha*, 'Delight'; *Starehe*, 'Comfort'; *Kivulini*, 'Shade'; 'Love-Boat Inn', 'Broadway', 'Cloud Nine', etc. Young people are hypnotized by the world of leisure, recreation and entertainment—by the stardom of stadium, stage or screen. This can encourage idleness, dissipation and delinquency, but there is no doubt also that young people want to be initiated into a life of which profitable and regular work is a part. Talk to almost any young man or woman in Nairobi, Kampala, Lusaka, Lagos or Kinshasa and they will relate a long story about their search for employment, about casual jobs they have had and about the frustrations they feel. In Nairobi the search for work is known as 'tarmacking', a term that vividly conjures up a process of endless street tramping. The Church has a well-established tradition of caring for young workers, but in the African town it is more appropriate to care for the unemployed. A centre for unemployed African youth might, in fact, be some kind of job centre, directing job-seekers to likely sources of employment, and advising them on training and other qualifications for work. Where labour exchanges exist in African cities, their scope is limited by the system of urban networks. The Church might help create an agency that would operate in a climate of confidence, matching jobs with real qualifications and vouching for the applicants it recommends.

Youth who leave home and family behind in the rural areas want to set up house on their own. They desperately want training for a secure and rewarding job. When these are not immediately available, they show considerable ingenuity and initiative in creating forms of self-employment. They are anxious to learn skills that will be useful to them. Leisure skills can also be profitable. Sport, for example, is often a recommendation for a job, since many companies have sports clubs and want to employ good footballers or good boxers and athletes. Besides which, boxing, athletics or football can introduce the young African into a world-culture of international travel and commercial opportunity. There is also money to be made in the bands that play in night-clubs, bars and hotels, and in the cultural and drama groups from which professionals are recruited for national dance and theatre companies. In working as market-carriers, bus touts, or truck-loaders, in running kiosks and food stalls, even in working as maize-roasters, peddlars or shoe-shine boys, the youth of African towns are offering services for which people are prepared to pay and are helping in the process of 'urbanization from below'.

The urban youth are often confused and disoriented morally. They lack stability and, indeed, any other purpose than the immediate one of making a living and enjoying life. Many would like to marry and have a stable family life, but many factors work against them. There are no accepted models of behaviour and no one to whom they can turn for advice. They experiment with relationships and lead a free sexual life. They are afraid of an indissoluble marriage union. They find themselves automatically becoming the 'Opposition Party' to the establishment and to their parents' generation. They are exploited and victimized in many ways, especially by a criminal code that favours vindictive and deterrent sentences. It is not surprising that the suicide rate among unemployed and under-employed urban youth is fairly high in African towns. It also explains why a number turn to alcohol, drugs or crime as a solution to their problems. Robbery, fraud and violence are short-cuts to the life of leisure to which many aspire, and they also serve other ideals, such as physical and sexual prowess, and skills of organization and resourcefulness. According to this mentality, all other values are subordinated to successful survival in the town.

As the Nairobi Churches Survey showed in 1986, the average age of those attending the city's worship centres is slightly lower than that of the city as a whole.[10] The Church is, therefore, meeting with some success in attracting the youth. Around 76 per cent of those attending church in Nairobi are under thirty years of age, and there is reason to believe that the pattern is similar in other African cities. Of the Catholic church-going youth, many are convinced of the need for prayer and a large proportion have made their first Communion and been confirmed. However, they look to the Church for special help in their situation, and there is no doubt that they find in it a social mechanism for improving their own position. They also find in the Church a moral code and rule of life that helps them withstand the temptations of criminality and moral disorientation. Adult guidance has to be maximized in an urban situation where the over-thirties are less than a quarter of the population. Youth problems abound, but the talents of youth are equally abundant. By recognizing and harnessing these talents, the Church is negotiating its best insurance for the future.

Pastoral care of students

University chaplaincies have the major task of drawing the connection between academic studies, on the one hand, and Christian faith and

117

commitment on the other. Their main task is to encourage the students to practise their faith through the conscientious exercise of the profession for which they are training. Students in African universities frequently live in a climate of contestation with the political authorities. Catholic chaplains have the task of protecting them as far as possible from extreme retaliation and of helping in the conciliation processes, without allowing student idealism to be compromised and without encouraging hooliganism and irresponsibility. Although their campus sometimes cuts them off from involvement in urban life, students are aware of the realities of social and political life. Medical, sociology and law students, in particular, are aware of the psychic, physical and social casualties of urban life. This is a fertile ground in which to sow the seeds of an active Christian commitment, and even to begin to address the injustices entailed by urbanization itself. University chaplaincies occasionally assume a national importance, as exponents of the Christian point of view on current issues. Their centres are frequented by the international elite, and their staff are sometimes in demand for broadcast or press interviews. All in all, university chaplaincies play an important part in the Church's urban mission in Africa.

Student centres are also a significant part of the Church's urban apostolate in Africa.[11] These cater for the large numbers of young people attending secondary schools in towns. Boarding schools and public hostels are often socially and morally uncongenial. They are also few in number, and many students stay with relatives or acquaintances in cramped and unsuitable conditions far away from their school. They finish school in the early afternoon, having had no food, and spend a long time getting back to their lodgings on public transport or on foot. On their return, they may be expected to perform household chores before settling down to study. Studying at home or in their lodgings, with poor light and few textbooks, also has its problems. In this situation, a student hostel with a library, study-room and sports facilities is extremely popular. Some Church-run hostels can even offer accommodation. Even ordinary urban parishes make their community centres available for evening study, and, in some parishes, teachers volunteer to give coaching lessons in the evening. However, the lack of security after dark often discourages students from taking full advantage of these facilities. Student centres and hostels exercise a stabilizing and integrating role, analogous to the parish itself. They also offer young people a place of their own and give them responsibilities in its running and maintenance.

Students and their parents look upon education as a form of

investment or 'banking' and all but a few dedicated teachers seem to ignore the moral aspect of their profession. It is up to the Church to ensure that Christian youth receive a requisite moral education. In Tanzania, some parishes appoint a *mshauri wa dini*, 'religious counsellor', or a *mlezi*, 'tutor', in the schools. However, teachers can be very authoritarian, and by modern Western standards disciplinary methods are often archaic. Much is done by religious education teams and through the Young Christian Students to inculcate moral standards and to help the youth develop a critical awareness of the society in which they live. A major drawback is the lack of liberal arts education and, in some countries, the overstress on political education. Some urban schools give agricultural teaching and have agricultural projects on the urban periphery. This is a welcome development, but it can do little to correct the over-all urban bias in African education. Student chaplaincies perform a useful function in the towns, but there is generally a need for the national co-ordination of student chaplaincies and student counselling, in view of the extreme mobility of the student population.

Youth activities in urban parishes

What is done for youth in urban parishes falls under four main headings: youth associations, choirs, sports and special activities. The Young Christian Students association everywhere enjoys considerable success. In Kenya alone there are more than 10,000 members. Because it operates at schools and colleges, and is promoted by specialist religion teachers and chaplains, it is assured of a continual follow-up and a continual adult reference and direction. Other youth associations tend not to be lasting. Often they are over-structured and make the young feel privileged, rather than inculcating a sense of service and responsibility. Many young people feel drawn, at one time or another, towards the ministry or religious life, and doubtless the social pressures of unemployment and economic uncertainty are contributory factors. It is a good thing to have an altar servers club or a vocations club in the parish to help sort out the genuine from the spurious vocations. In organizing these, the girls should not be neglected, even though they are less numerous than the boys and less available.

Church choirs flourish in every African town. The youth are keen on them and they take the form of a club with extracurricular activities, such as parties, outings, dances, drama, musical competitions, song composition and recording. In Catholic parishes one

119

frequently finds three or four choirs which sing at the different Masses. There is a considerable exchange of choir membership among the different town parishes, and singers and instrumentalists may travel some distance in order to participate in the regular activities of a prestigious choir. Choir members exhibit a fair degree of professionalism. The choirs have the opportunity of broadcasting on radio or television, and of performing publicly in hotels, halls and shopping-centres. They have their own meetings and social life. Competitions are organized between parish choirs. For example, in several African towns one encounters Catholic Choirs Associations that organize such competitions, and co-ordinate activities when massed choirs are needed for special occasions. The choirs teach musical instruments as well as singing, and there is considerable creativity and musical composition. This received extensive encouragement in the Catholic Church after the introduction of the vernacular liturgy. Gospel songs and social songs are also composed. Some choirs run jazz bands as well. Sometimes the external activities of choirs tend to swallow up their parish activities, and there is a constant struggle to ensure that their enthusiasm, professionalism and outside commitments do not operate to the detriment of the parish liturgy for which they exist and which they are intended to serve.

In my experience, surprisingly few parishes have sports clubs, or sponsor their own sports teams. Those that do so have been highly successful. An example is the *Chipukizi* ('Young Plant') Sports Club in Tabora town, Tanzania, which has its own club premises and sports field and which boasts of having defeated the Tanzanian Army Football team. In Eastleigh Catholic Parish, Nairobi, the Boxing and Karate Clubs have enjoyed appreciable success. Several international boxers have emerged from the parish and at least one Nairobi champion. The clubs have their own managers and run their own affairs. Their training classes bring a great many young people to the parish compound. A number of members have found employment in the postal service, the breweries or the armed forces, because of their sporting prowess. The deanery 'Olympics' or youth festivals that are held in the Eastlands Catholic Deanery of Nairobi provide another focus for parish youth activities. A typical youth festival includes football and netball competitions, drama, poetry recitation, dancing competitions, a filmshow, and finally a disco. In the absence of other forms of organization, the parish and deanery structures are able to articulate such activities between different areas of the town, and draw the young people together.

Special youth activities include seminars, evening schools, Bible study, drama clubs and youth days (e.g. *Pax Christi, Carrefours*). Often young people respond enthusiastically to the challenge of an all-night vigil, a charity walk or a pilgrimage. The *Bilenge ya Mwinda*, 'Youth of Light', is a movement started in the early 1970s by Father Matondo Kwa Nzambi, in one of the poorest areas of Kinshasa City, Zaire.[12] Through this movement, the Christian youth aim to reawaken the faith of their parents and elders. They have, in effect, been co-opted by the parish team for the work of re-evangelization. The movement makes use of traditional ideas of initiation for inducting members into the various stages of commitment. The Youth of Light movement has now spread to English-speaking East Africa and is very popular with young people.

In view of the overwhelming numbers of young people in urban parishes, it is essential that they should be involved in parish activities. It is an excellent idea to have a parish youth council that brings together representatives of all the different youth activities, and that is represented, in its turn, on the parish pastoral council. Young people should, if possible, take full part in the basic ecclesial communities, but sometimes they are not welcomed by the adults who provide the leadership. For this reason, it is necessary that the youth have their own organizations and structures, on the basis of which they can relate to the communities and the other parish structures. When the Youth of Light was founded in Kinshasa, they visited the basic communities and secured their co-operation for their re-evangelization campaign.[13] A similar 'Young Adults Association' or 'Young Christians Association' can provide the necessary springboard. For two years, 1984–85, I acted as chaplain to the Mathare Young Christians Society in Nairobi's principal squatter area. This group had its own activities: prayer, Bible reading, sport, drama, poetry and singing. But they also contributed to parish activities, by helping out at the foster homes for street youngsters and contributing to the parish liturgies. There is no reason why young people should not also have their representatives among the parish officials, for example the church ushers, the justice and peace committee, the catechists, and even the Eucharistic ministers. The enormous preponderance of youth in the African urban parish must be confronted with inventiveness and great realism.

Some of the special urban apostolates that are described in the chapter that follows also concern the under-thirties. This is especially the case with the industrial apostolate. However, in the African city it is necessary, as we have suggested in this chapter, to meet the youth on their own terms, as a distinctive and significant stratum of the urban population.

References

1 An earlier version of this story appeared in *The Catholic Leader*, Brisbane, Australia, 24 March 1985, p. 6.

2 For much of this section I am indebted to Dallape 1987.

3 Cf. Mayer 1970; Fontaine 1970.

4 Dallape 1987, pp. 41–42.

5 The Undugu Society of Kenya has an excellent agricultural training centre at Kitangi, not far from Nairobi City.

6 Dallape 1987, pp. 104–8.

7 Ibid.

8 In Ki-Swahili, *vijana*, for example.

9 For a discussion of the pastoral care of urban and rural youth in Africa, cf. Tessier 1983 and Tessier 1984.

10 Downes *et al.* 1989, p. 37.

11 During my 1982–83 research, I visited three such centres in Tanzania at Dar es Salaam, Tabora and Mbeya.

12 Father Matondo Kwa Nzambi is now the Catholic Bishop of Basankusu.

13 Tessier 1983, p. 67.

10

Ecumenism and special urban apostolates

Inter-Church co-operation in a Zimbabwe town

Bulawayo, in south-west Zimbabwe, is the tribal capital of the Nde-
bele. When I first visited the city at the end of August 1970, it was
a fine, basically European, town, with wide streets and public buildings
of grey granite. Attractive 'white' suburbs blazed with bougainvillea
and flamboyants, and on the outskirts lay the sprawling African
locations, with their corrugated iron roofs and their dusty surrounds.
At the time of my visit, Bulawayo was the setting for a remarkable
experiment in ecumenical co-operation that was just about to flower.[1]
Like most African towns of the period, Bulawayo had embarked on
a period of expansion resulting from migration from the surrounding
rural areas. By the mid-1960s Zimbabwe's urban level stood at close
to 20 per cent. The migrants brought their church affiliations with
them and the African townships averaged between twenty and forty
different religious congregations. Six or seven years before my visit,
the African Christian Workers' Fraternal had been founded for
workers of divergent Protestant denominations, and a measure of co-
operation had been achieved in school religion teaching, hospital work
and prison services. The ACWF was most successful in maintaining
an inter-racial membership, although most of the white clergy preferred to join the Bulawayo Ministers' Fraternal, which was almost
exclusively white.

I had experienced something of Bulawayo's inter-racial problems
during my visit, the purpose of which was to preach at a weekend
retreat organized by the Catholic parishes of the city. Of the sixty or

so retreatants, twelve were coloureds and only four were Africans. The rest were white. The ACWF's achievement was the more remarkable, therefore, and it was not surprising that the initiative was soon accompanied by the launching of the Bulawayo Council of Churches, uniting ten Protestant denominations. In 1967, the Roman Catholic bishops sent two observers to the meeting of the national Christian Council and four Catholic dioceses were represented at the National Urban Consultation in the following year. The year before I visited Bulawayo, a Catholic priest had been co-opted by the executive of the Bulawayo Council of Churches and Catholics began to take part in the action groups it had set up in the town. Chief among these was Joint Action Bulawayo, which offered leadership training courses in the African townships, sponsored post-primary education, and launched a campaign to improve housing conditions. It also became involved in youth work and in aid to the families of political detainees.

The Bulawayo experience undoubtedly received encouragement from the 1961 General Assembly of the World Council of Churches in New Delhi and the Second Vatican Council which was meeting in Rome in the early 1960s. It was also a united Christian response to the worsening political situation under the regime of Ian Smith, a situation that was shortly to develop into civil war, the murder of Bishop Adolf Schmitt (Catholic Bishop of Bulawayo at the time of my visit), and the long struggle with the dissidents after independence. However, this ecumenism, exceptional and hopeful as it was, took the almost exclusive form of issue-oriented action groups and had little success in melting the institutional rigidity of the member Churches.[2] Its interest lies in the practical character and urban context of its activities. In this chapter we shall examine the opportunities for ecumenism that the African town offers and some of the special apostolates that invite ecumenical co-operation.

Ecumenism in the African town

The missionaries of the divergent Christian denominations in Africa traditionally operated out of rurally based headquarters, and their rural spheres of interest were carefully delineated and distanced from one another. When their Christian adepts moved to the towns, the Churches found themselves in unaccustomed proximity, and their self-incapsulation began to be perceived as a stumbling-block. This is especially true of the shanty-towns where as many as thirty or forty denominations worship and witness in isolation from one another, and carry on in every respect as if the others did not exist. If the

124

Churches were genuinely committed to Christian unity, they would regard the urban presence of numerous denominations as a heaven-sent opportunity. Such, alas, is not the case. The Bulawayo experience is still very much an exception. Geographical isolation in the country-side is replaced by mental isolation in the town.

If ecumenism enjoys any success, it is at the academic level, which is usually less threatening. For eight years I belonged to an ecumenical discussion group in Kampala City, Uganda. This group united representatives of the town-based theological colleges and Church institutions, as well as members of the university department of religious studies. Most of us were Catholics or Anglicans and we achieved a remarkable consensus in discussing the agreed statements of the Anglican–Roman Catholic International Commission. Many of us were teaching in one another's establishments and some were co-operating in the publication of a joint religious education syllabus for secondary schools. Apart from this, I do not believe that we made any impact on Uganda, its capital city or the structures and leadership of our various Churches.

Ecumenical reluctance in the African town may be a symptom of the urban privatization of religion. Worse still, it may contribute to the growth of a secular attitude and a conviction that religion is irrelevant to the city's problems. In fact, religious pluralism in the African city produces many problems of its own: changes of affiliation, playing the religion 'supermarket', inter-Church marriages. Even when the denominations turn in upon themselves, these problems do not go away. They have to be faced jointly. Equally, however, the urban situation presents the Churches with opportunities for learning about one another and for sharing in worship and witness. Preachers in some denominations spend a great deal of time 'rubbishing' other Churches during their sermons. This is less easy to do in town where the veracity of their attacks can be immediately tested by going to the Church in question and seeing for oneself. The proximity of the various denominations makes ecumenical understanding and co-oper-ation much easier, but this very facility appears threatening to some, particularly those whose members are insufficiently instructed. The Churches on the whole remain authoritarian and tightly controlled and this severely inhibits their promotion of Christian unity.

There are limits also to the development of ecumenical struc-tures, such as Christian Councils. These rarely include Roman Cath-olics and conservative Evangelicals, and almost never involve indigen-ous Christian movements. Catholics, with their large numbers, may either be uninterested in ecumenical activity, or fearful of precipitating the departure from the Council of Protestants who object to their membership. For many conservative Evangelicals, ecumenism is not a priority at all. Their anxiety is to safeguard the purity of the Bible Christianity they profess against other denominations whom they regard as having placed it in jeopardy. The new indigenous movements or 'Independent Churches' are somewhat anti-structural and have a vested interest in the proliferation of small groups that offer a holistic experience to their members. Their membership is fluid and usually mono-ethnic. They have little in common with the mainline Churches, and, unlike them, they hold an appeal for the urban and peri-urban poor because of their informality and ethnic cultural affiliations. It is obvious that the Churches have much to learn from one another in addressing the problems of urban dwellers, and although associations of Independent Churches are coming into being, it may not always be through inter-Church councils that co-operation is best articulated. Lessons can be learned, perhaps, from the experience of black-led Churches in Britain and the United States.

Probably the best approach is that of the joint action group which proved such a success in Bulawayo. Churches can co-operate in social planning and research, in relief work, education, housing and health care and they can act together more effectively on social justice issues. There is more likelihood of growing together and learning from one another through such joint action than through academic discussion or contacts among leaders at the highest levels. If such joint action becomes a growing reality, then the chances are that joint worship in the Christian Unity Octave, or participating in each other's city events, congresses, conventions, missions and crusades, will become more meaningful.

Indigenous religious movements

It is worth taking a closer look at the indigenous movements or Independent Churches, since the gulf between them and mainline Christianity is a difficult one to bridge. In many ways they are more successful than the mainline Churches in acting as adaptive social mechanisms for the urban migrant. Their doctrine is often at variance with that of mainstream Christianity, placing greater emphasis on the Old Testament and holding a weak and sometimes ambiguous Christology. Their strength lies in their ethnic character, their reinterpretation of ethnic culture, their community experience and the mental framework within which newcomers to the town can cope with a potentially threatening situation. As a rule, they attract members from among the poorer and more marginal sections of the population, and they flourish in the shanty-towns and squatter areas of African cities.

It is not easy for indigenous movements and mainline Churches to relate to one another. For one thing, the former tend not to be interested in promoting Christian unity. For another, they tend to be somewhat closed to outside influences. Although they have a fluctuating fellowship, their only interest in outside relationships tends to be that of attracting new members to their own community. When their members become more sophisticated—that is, when their education and salaries improve—they tend to join the mainline Churches, rather than to remain with the indigenous movements on the street corners and open spaces of the low-income areas. Their mobility of membership is responsible for the spread of adventist and faith-healing ideas and practices that are sometimes difficult to reconcile with traditional Christian teaching.

The mainline Churches are burdened with monolithic structures and ecclesiastical bureaucracy. Their large congregations often render them impersonal and their worship makes few concessions to local African culture. It is clear that, if they are to cater for the majority of the urban poor, they must both emulate the indigenous movements and enter into relations with them. Adopting a communities-based structure, inculturating worship and organizing open-air services may recommend them to the poorer classes, but will make them competitors of the Independent Churches. A breakthrough might be possible through a shared experience of charismatic prayer, but the charismatic movement in the mainline Churches is often in the hands of a religious elite. Once again, it seems that the ecumenical road lies in joint social action. There is ultimately no substitute for personal contacts among leaders, for consultation and shared strategies to alleviate the condition of the urban poor.

Inter-faith co-operation

The various faiths of the immigrant communities in African towns and cities are usually co-terminous with the race and culture of those who profess them. They include Judaism, Hinduism, Sikhism, Ismaeli Islam and Baha'i. There is limited proselytism and little opportunity for inter-religious dialogue. However, Christian leaders should inform themselves about these religions, and they should also try to encourage the adherents to carry out social and philanthropic action, especially since they are mostly members of the business community. The work of Mother Teresa of Calcutta and her Missionaries of Charity in the slums of African cities is proving to be a focal point for joint social action with Asian members of other faiths.

The main religion with which Christians have to contend in the towns and cities of Africa is Islam and the oldest and most committed group of town dwellers in Africa are Muslims. They form a strong and cohesive social network. In East Africa, especially Kenya, urban low-income areas contain many Somali-owned shops. There are also small Nubian communities in the cities of East Africa. In these groups, religion reinforces ethnic identity. Urban Muslims tend to specialize in particular forms of business, such as the butchery trade, or long-distance bus driving. According to the Shafi law, which African Muslims in East Africa follow, a Christian woman may only retain her faith on marriage to a Muslim if her ancestors were 'people of the book' at the time of Muhammad. This obviously excludes all Africans, and so any Christian woman who marries a Muslim is obliged to change her faith. Muslim women are never allowed to marry a Christian. This marriage law makes inter-faith marriages operate exclusively in favour of Islam and tends to strengthen the Muslim community. It is often the cause of much bitterness and suffering for those who are involved.

Informal contact and social relationships with Muslims are possible, but there are few opportunities for formal inter-religious dialogue. In recent years, Arab countries, such as Libya and Saudi Arabia, have spent a great deal of money in black Africa, building mosques and schools and training teachers and missionaries. As a result of this, Muslims have become more aggressive.[3] Sometimes Christians have been invited to explain their beliefs to groups of Muslims, and this has occasionally developed into an unhelpful polemical exchange. Biblical and Qur'anic texts have been bandied to and fro, and considerably more heat than light has been generated. Christians should not allow themselves to be lured into such debates without a thorough knowledge of the Islamic positions that underlie the Muslim's approach to the Christian Bible. Especially, they should not attempt to counter one type of fundamentalism with another.

An indirect approach that has been explored by the Mennonite Church in Nairobi is that of a Bible correspondence course for Muslims. The latter's knowledge of the Christian Bible is often limited to the proof-texts of Islamic aplogetics. The correspondence course is attractive because it enables them to learn more about the personalities of both the Old and the New Testaments who are mentioned in the Koran, without the distraction of religious controversy. Once again,

128

social action probably provides the best ambience in which Christians and Muslims can come to understand and respect one another.

African ethnic religions, as one would expect, are well represented in urban areas, particularly through traditional healers, diviners, mediums and witch-finders. However, these practitioners tend to be more reticent towards Christians and Christian leaders than in the rural areas, and often, for the sake of respectability, they adopt titles such as 'Professor', 'Doctor' or 'Sheikh' and operate 'clinics', 'hospitals' or 'surgeries'. Herbal medicine is emphasized in town as being more scientific and respectable, especially since Western medical foundations have launched projects of research into them. In the urban situation, African healing traditions are increasingly linked to Western lore, in the shape of casting horoscopes or the application of numerology. Indeed, African traditional medicine is highly syncretist. Dialogue is often possible with urban exponents of African traditional religion, and an example is provided by Dr Kalibala of Kampala who took part in the 1975 Vatican consultation on African Religions.[4]

Industrial missions

A growing number of urban dwellers in Africa are employed in industry. This can take the form of mining, manufacturing, processing or construction, and there are expanding industrial areas in most African cities and towns. Although these are necessarily situated within the borders of particular urban parishes, it is unrealistic to expect the ordinary parish to run an industrial mission on its own, unless its industrial area is relatively small. In St Matia Mulumba's Catholic Parish, Thika (Kenya), and Manzese Catholic Parish, Dar es Salaam (Tanzania), there are a few factories and the workers live close at hand within the parish boundaries. It has therefore been possible to organize the Christian factory workers through basic communities and to attempt to negotiate better salaries and conditions of work, as well as to tackle environmental pollution created by the factories.[5] In other instances a parish may have a limited number of residents, but literally hundreds of thousands of industrial workers who live elsewhere and commute to factories in the parish. On the principle that interparochial structures are needed to cope with typically urban problems, it is clear that an industrial mission is far from being a luxury, especially where workers reside in another parish. Such a mission would benefit from being ecumenical because this would carry greater weight with employers and employees alike. It would also help the pastors to share information, responsibilities and even, possibly, expenses.

While it is comparatively easy to visit parishioners in markets, offices or shops, it is more difficult to do so on the factory or workshop floor. Factory-floor visits may be instructive for the pastors, but they are not the occasion for much pastoral work. More can be done in the lunch hour. Many African workers do not spend much time on lunch. Sprawled on the grass verges outside the factory or workshop gates, they provide a ready audience for the lunch-hour preachers who abound in cities like Nairobi, Dar es Salaam, Kinshasa or Harare. In Africa as a whole Protestants have led the way in urban–industrial consultation and planning. Prompted by the Tanzanian government's report on the Dar es Salaam Master Plan in 1967, Lloyd Swantz of the Lutheran Evangelical Church spearheaded the Dar es Salaam Urban–Industrial Project for the Christian Council of Tanzania. This advocated joint planning for all the religious denominations in the city. In Jinja, Uganda, the Anglican Church of Uganda launched an active industrial mission, while in Kenya the Eastern Africa Urban Committee, one of three regional bodies set up by the All Africa Council of Churches (AACC), held an urban consultation in 1972. The Baptist Daystar University College has been carrying out urban research in Nairobi since the mid-1980s.[6] The Catholic Church has been slower than most others to organize industrial consultations and missions, or even to gain access to factory canteens and to organize lunch-hour meetings, but it was the National Urban Consultation in Zimbabwe that precipitated Catholic participation in the Bulawayo Council of Churches in 1969. In 1974 the Catholic Bishops' Association in Eastern Africa (AMECEA) joined with the AACC to organize a nine-month seminar on Urban and Industrial Concerns in Kenya, and this was subsequently reflected in the resolutions of Catholic diocesan synods and other gatherings.[7] On the whole, the impression gained is that practice in most Churches lags behind theoretical discussion on industrial questions. In one region of Africa, however, the Church has committed itself very extensively to the industrial mission. This is in the Republic of South Africa, where Catholic and other Christian missionaries have followed migrant workers from Malawi, Lesotho and the Bantu homelands to the great urban mining complexes of Johannesburg and the Transvaal. There they have tried to ameliorate the inhuman labour system, by teaching workers their rights, by facilitating family visits, and improving working and safety conditions.

The worker-priest movement after the Second World War was an attempt—mainly in France—to communicate with the alienated working class. It fell foul of Church authorities, and nothing like it was ever considered relevant to Africa. The Young Christian Workers was another movement started in Belgium for young Catholics in industry. This has been brought to Africa, but it has been argued that in Africa it is more urgent to cater for the young Christian unemployed and to assist in job creation, to sponsor job-centres and day-centres for job-seekers. Everything has to be done pastorally, through catechesis and liturgy to help the unemployed feel that the Christian community is actively concerned for them and that God himself helps them in their struggle to survive. However, a properly organized industrial mission, with its own chaplains, is certainly also a growing need. It could operate on the scale of the city itself, or that of the deanery, or even nationally, in much the same way that student centres do in Tanzania. Such a mission could become a major spearhead against the exploitation of cheap labour in African towns, especially by foreign businesses.

Other special apostolates

Among other specialized chaplaincies and apostolates, there are two interparochial services that are of the utmost importance in town: medicine and prisons. Large, regional hospitals are found in town, serving not only the massive urban population, but also the people on the periphery of the town. Townspeople often bring their sick relatives to urban hospitals from remote rural areas. There are also innumerable private clinics operating in towns. It is impossible for a parish to accept sole responsibility for a large hospital, merely because it happens to be on its territory. Some parishes have several hospitals within their borders and large numbers of clinics. A large city or town should have its own medical–pastoral team, with priests on call. Such a team normally has the confidence of the medical staff themselves. This specialized team keeps a record of seriously ill or long-term patients, ministers regularly to them, and communicates with their churches or parishes of origin.

In the district township of Sengerema, Tanzania, which I visited in 1982 as part of the research on which this book is based, I found a full-time hospital chaplain in the district hospital. It is rare that a hospital enjoys the services of a full-time chaplain. This is the result of several causes. In the first place the hospital was originally a Catholic hospital run by a nursing order, the Brothers of St John of God. In the second place it is a reasonably small district hospital. Finally, the chaplain at the time of my research had a disability himself, which meant that he could not undertake normal parish work.

131

As a result, this chaplaincy provided a model of what could be achieved in this field.

Sengerema hospital is part of the government regional medical system which has its headquarters at Bugando hospital, Mwanza. The hospital, including maternity wards, has 250 beds. Patients come from all over the district and Sengerema townspeople are the most numerous among the out-patients. There were five doctors at the time of my visit, one of whom was district medical officer of health. There were twenty male trainee nurses and eighty female trainees in the nurses' training school. This offered a three-year basic training course, plus a fourth year for midwifery. Trainees come from all over Tanzania. In the regional medical assistants' school, a two-year upgrading course was being followed by eighty men, rural medical aides now in the process of becoming medical assistants capable of running a health centre. Two of the doctors taught in the RMA school and there are also two full-time teachers and a religious sister on the staff of the nurses' training school.

The chaplain looked after patients, staff and trainees. He gave a medical ethics course in both training schools.[8] Mass was celebrated on Sunday afternoon for the whole hospital community. Among the patients at any one time there were about thirty Catholics, fifty Christians of other denominations, and ten Muslims. The chaplain visited all patients every day and returned to those who wished to pray with him or receive the sacraments. Quite often non-Christians, even Muslims, asked for prayers. An Anglican priest visited the patients of his communion, but the other denominations were not frequent in their visits. Pentecostals tended to come only to distribute tracts. The chaplain was a full member of the hospital staff and worked closely with them. He was often entrusted with the task of breaking the news to terminally ill patients.

Various methods have been devised of bringing joy and hope to the patients in Sengerema Hospital. A group of sister-aspirants visited the wards in the afternoons and sang songs for a few minutes. The patients eagerly looked forward to these visits. The chaplain also had a library of 500 books in Swahili for the patients and a library of recreational and spiritual books for the trainees. A sound system has been set up with loudspeakers in all except the isolation wards. Daily and morning prayers were broadcast on the system, a short news broadcast from Radio Tanzania, and pre-recorded talks on health and hygiene in Swahili and Ki-Sukuma. From time to time there were music programmes. Other Churches were invited to broadcast prayers and hymns of their own.

The Churches are frequently involved in health-care projects, particularly in the shanty-towns and lower-income areas of African cities. Today, there is a growing need for hospital-based AIDS programmes. These provide centres for diagnosis and counselling, education and publicity and, where possible, a hospice for debilitated patients. Examples of AIDS programmes based on hospitals in African towns are those of Mzuzu, Malawi and Kitovu, Uganda.

Another service, usually organized on a national scale, is that of prison chaplains. Where very large numbers of young offenders are held on remand, or are picked up by police without the knowledge of their relatives, it is important to have this specialized ministry. After conviction, life in the archaic prisons of Africa can be bleak and brutalizing. Many people from the urban squatter areas are condemned to long terms of imprisonment, often on the flimsiest of evidence. The illegal character of the shanty-town makes it more or less inevitable that large numbers become involved in crime. Suspected offenders are constantly being picked up by the police and relatives need help to trace them and follow up their cases. Prison chaplains and Christian prison associations keep in touch with the prison populations, build up prison libraries, help to organize trade courses or other study programmes, and generally show that God has not abandoned them. They can then prepare the parishes and families to receive them back and, if possible, help them find employment. Chaplains do what they can pastorally for those on death row. Once again, full-time chaplains and pastoral teams are required. Care for prisoners, who come from all over the country, cannot be the responsibility of the local parish alone.

Mission to seamen and fishermen

Many African cities are also ports for sea-going ships and there is a need for a specialized apostolate to seamen and fishermen. In Dar es Salaam the Catholic Apostleship of the Sea has been integrated with the Anglican Mission to Seamen.[9] This mission is situated near the port area and, although it belongs to the Anglican Church of Tanzania, it is headed by a priest of the Church of England, assisted by a Tanzanian Anglican priest. The mission is called 'The Flying Angel Club' and has a bar, restaurant, co-operative shop, swimming-pool, football pitch and other recreational facilities. The Catholic chaplain says Mass in the chapel there and there is a lay volunteer who helps in the running of the club. The club, however, is for the exclusive use of seamen from the big ships that call at Dar es Salaam. It does not cater for local sailors.

For two out of every three weeks the harbour berths are full, but every now and then, as a result of the falling-off of imports, the port is seemingly empty. About 40,000 sailors come to the mission each year. The Anglican chaplains visit the English-speaking ships and the Catholic chaplain visits the non-English-speaking vessels. These include the French ships and the 'flag of convenience' ships. The latter are increasing and many ships are becoming Asian-crewed as an economy measure. The chaplains visit the ships in the outer anchorage and also those at the oil terminal on the seaward side of Kigamboni headland. Services are held on board ship when they are asked for.

The Catholic chaplain possesses a mini-bus and a dinghy called *Nyota ya Bahari*, 'Star of the Sea'. There are more than 11,000 dock-workers in the port, which serves Tanzania, Zambia, Rwanda, Burundi and Zaire. Although the dockers are not technically included in the orbit of the mission to seamen, there are inevitable welfare cases in which there is no one to help but the chaplain. Sailors from abroad have a bad reputation for obscenities, nudity and loose morals, but this is far from being always deserved. The seamen's club was planned for rich, Western seamen whose ships are 'floating palaces' in the eyes of the poor Tanzanian sailors and fishermen. For this reason, the Catholic chaplain's apostolate has been extended to these latter.

The nomads of the sea are the dhow people, and the Dar es Salaam dhow wharf may have up to twenty Lamu dhows or *jahazis* tied up. These are the ancient wooden sailing ships of the East African coast. There are also trawlers and schooners (dhows with in-board engines). Dhow traffic is popular because their operating costs are cheaper than those of ships with engines, though nowadays only the local craft from Pemba, Zanzibar, Mafia, Kilwa Kivinje and Songo-Songo are seen. In 1974, 1,416 dhows put into Dar es Salaam; in 1975 this figure rose to 2,122.[10] Apart from the captain, or *narodha*, and his mate, dhow crews consist of young men. They number about twelve to each vessel. In port the captain goes in search of a cargo — diesel oil, vegetables, rice, cement, soft drinks, flour, beer and so forth. While the cargo is being assembled, the young crew members roam the streets. The chaplain has succeeded in setting up a recreational centre and hostel for them near the port. The authorities, however, have an ambivalent attitude towards dhows. They accuse them, with some justice, of being unsafe, but they also suspect them of smuggling and drug-peddling. Dhow crews are Muslims and many of the youngsters aspire to become deck-hands on a big ship.

Farther along the harbour shore are the mainly motorized fishing-smacks, or *mashua*. About 100 are regularly beached there and the whole *mashua* population is around 500. The majority are young men from up-country, many of them Christians. Quite a few have had some experience on board a big ship and they aspire to this type of work. The crew of a fishing-smack is around seven at most. Farther along the shore, beyond the fish-market, are the out-rigger *ngalawa*, or canoes with sails. They give employment to about 450 people, mostly young Muslims with homes in Dar es Salaam.

This special apostolate consists in contact, pre-evangelization and first evangelization. It includes collaborating with the Tanzanian National Union of Seamen and the Seamen's Mission in providing these youngsters with further chances of training in the profession of their choice. Most do not qualify for entry to the Marine Training Unit nor do they have the sponsorship of one of Tanzania's three shipping lines or the harbour authority. The chaplain has set up courses at the Seamen's Mission. These include an elementary seamanship course leading to a certificate as able seaman and a course on safety at sea, with dhows especially in mind. He has also set up a co-operative that runs its own affairs and that can deal with all the authorities involved. An office has been opened where Tanzanian seamen and fishermen who are denied access to the Seamen's Mission can be received. This affords a base for counselling and welfare. The attempt is thus being made to bridge the gap between the informal seamanship sector and the officially accepted, though foreign, world of the sea, from which young Tanzanian seamen are alienated and excluded. The Seamen's Mission now realizes its responsibilities and has generously co-operated in fund-raising for welfare and in loaning premises for the courses.

In the foregoing chapters of this book we have considered a whole range of facts and trends in African urbanization and in the Church's response to this striking contemporary phenomenon. We have examined urban growth and the rural–urban continuum in Africa. We have investigated the social forms of urban life and the growth of squatter settlements. We have looked at the Church's urban mission and structures, and the special apostolates of the African city, particularly the pastoral care of urban youth. In the final chapter we draw some practical conclusions for the Church's future involvement in the towns and cities of Africa.

References

1 Cf. Thomas 1975, pp. 240–46.

2 Ibid., p. 251.

3 Much of the Muslim–Christian controversy in East Africa has centred on the spurious *Gospel of Barnabas*, which generally constitutes an important plank of Islamic propaganda.

4 Cf. *Bulletin*, Secretariat for Non-Christians, 1975–X/1, 28–29, pp. 101–73.

5 Cf. Max Stetter in Tessier 1983, pp. 73–82; Tessier 1984, pp. 56–60; also in Peil 1982, pp. 76–87.

6 Cf. Downes *et al.* 1989.

7 The author contributed to this seminar at Limuru Conference Centre.

8 This is now published as *Maadili ya Uganda*. See A. Broos 1988.

9 This account is based on a study of the mission carried out at the end of 1982. At that time the Catholic chaplain was Father George Loire MAfr. Since 1988 his place has been taken by Father Gerard Tronche MAfr.

10 These figures are quoted by Martin 1978, p. 121.

11

Urbanization: today's missionary reality in Africa

Anti-urbanism and the urban bias

In an early play entitled *The Swamp Dwellers*, the Nigerian playwright and Nobel prize-winner Wole Soyinka depicts the city in Africa with prophetical pessimism.[1] It is a great brass monster that swallows up the younger generation. Those who succeed in the city are lost forever. They are, to all intents and purposes, dead. Those who fail are regurgitated into the surrounding swamps, the wastelands that the city has created in the rural areas. It is a poignant, if pessimistic, picture. The naïve urban bias of the youngster who is attracted to the city is contrasted with the anti-urban despair he leaves behind him in the homeland, and which he eventually comes to share on his return. He is caught between 'one slough and another'. His twin brother, on the other hand, has won success in the city—at a price. The price is that he has had to set his back on humanity itself. If Soyinka's picture is ultimately pessimistic, it is not crudely anti-urban. Success in the city is not impossible. What is frightening is the effect that the city has on the peri-urban surroundings, on the human rejects that it casts aside and, above all, on the dehumanized urban rich that it cherishes.

In Africa today members of the younger generation display a frenzied urban bias, while the Church struggles lethargically to shake off its toils of anti-urbanism. Both extremes of urban bias and anti-urbanism are unrealistic in the circumstances. Urbanization is a reality that cannot be wished away. It is a concomitant of human history, human culture and human economic development. In the final analysis, however, it is an unjust reality in contemporary Africa—the producer and product of systematic injustice. Urbanization is not merely an abstraction bandied about by sociologists and anthropologists in learned debate. It is an urgent, life or death issue for all of us—for humanity and for the Church. It is useless for the priest or pastor, the missionary or church-worker, the catechist or the community leader, to tread water, as it were, while waiting for a life-saver to appear on the beach. They must strike out at once for the shore. In other words, it is no good waiting for an urban specialist to drop in to cope with these new problems. We ourselves are usually the only available specialists and it is up to us to confront the gigantic dilemma that urbanization poses in Africa and in the world at large.

There are at least four reasons why urbanization is a life or death issue. These can be stated as follows: (1) Urbanization pollutes. (2) Urbanization impoverishes. (3) Urbanization disorientates. (4) Urbanization secularizes.

Urbanization and pollution

Industry is mostly urban based and is one of the major sources of environmental pollution. This is true of both mining and manufacturing industries. The mines throw up hazardous mountains of waste material, while the mining process itself endangers the miners' health. Factories pollute the atmosphere and the water supply, covering the neighbourhood with a coating of dust, soot and chemical sediment. Sometimes lethal effluents and gases are released by factories that affect the health of a population over several generations. Bhopal in India is a terrible lesson in this respect. In many African slums petrol tankers are parked at night in the narrow alleys and constitute a terrifying fire risk. Fifteen years ago, in the Kampala slum of Kisenyi, a petrol tanker exploded, sending burning fuel down the streets and drains, causing a conflagration out of all proportion to the initial blast, which was serious enough in itself.

Urbanization pollutes through its massive slum conurbations, the shanty and squatter outgrowths of African cities, with their inhuman and insanitary conditions, their refuse heaps and their lack of adequate drainage and water. These areas propagate diseases, epidemics and infections of all kinds: dysentery, cholera, meningitis, pneumonia and many other illnesses. Slum dwellers are more exposed also to the possibility of fires and traffic accidents. Automobiles are also concentrated in the cities and their emissions pollute the atmosphere and constitute a health risk for urban dwellers, especially children. Urbanization ultimately pollutes the rural areas, through absentee landlord-

138

ism, bureaucratization of farming, the degradation of farmland by urban-based exploiters, and the deforestation caused by urban consumption of fuelwood and charcoal.[2] Rural development projects in food or cash crops fail because urban-based ruling elites pay farmers prices that are too low to provide an incentive to make better use of resources.[3]

Improving material conditions of living and rescuing the environment are natural concerns of Christianity. Sean McDonagh has argued persuasively that the theology of salvation must learn to link the continuing redemption of human beings with the redemption of the earth.[4] We should not have such a heightened emphasis on otherworldly salvation that we are blind to the destruction of God's creation and to condemning every succeeding generation to squalor and poverty. A major goal for the Church in the town is to convince people that resources should be husbanded, safely exploited, and fairly shared. Julius Nyerere, former President of Tanzania, exhorted the Church to fight those institutions and power groups that contribute to the existence and maintenance of physical and spiritual slums, and it is perfectly true that physical and moral degradation tend to reinforce one another in the town.[5] It is precisely because there is nothing saintly about imposed poverty that we recognize the heroism of those who manage to rise above their demoralizing environment. Besides helping to effect a change of heart, therefore, the Church has to effect a change in human living conditions, in sanitation, hygiene, health care, and the provision of building materials.

Urbanization and poverty

The continuing flood of urban migrants in Africa produces a kind of social erosion that widens the gulf between rich and poor. It favours human exploitation, under-employment, inequitable remuneration and unjust working conditions. The migrant becomes a non-person, a surplus individual, an illegal and unwanted intruder in the eyes of the affluent, established urban dweller. A situation has developed in the cities and towns of Africa that, if it is not apartheid in a racist sense, is analogous to apartheid. Urban migrants supply labour to all the economic sectors of the city. They are largely responsible for feeding the city, and they provide innumerable services to the city's population. Yet they are not accorded equal rights with the city's affluent members. Amenities are not equably shared and there is a gross disproportion between the remuneration and prospects of the minority, compared to those of the majority. Towns and cities are essentially mechanisms for the creation and distribution of wealth, but in Africa the wealth generated by urbanization is unevenly distributed and this anomaly is growing, rather than diminishing. Employers profit from the cheap labour that massive urban migration provides, while, paradoxically, trying to keep the reservoir of cheap labour at a distance and denying it full urban citizenship and full remuneration. Urban squatters are harassed in innumerable ways. They can be evicted without mercy and their dwellings can be demolished without redress. This amounts ineluctably to a system of internal colonialism.

In so far as money, jobs, goods and services trickle down from the circle of the affluent, they are channelled through urban networks of patronage. This produces a wasteful, uneconomic and unjust system which denies ordinary clients and customers their rights, and which contributes to the erosion of social justice in the city. It also has the effect of increasing the wealth and influence of the affluent patrons themselves.

Peri-urbanization, urban primacy and the urban bias extend this internal colonialism to the rural areas. This is because urban migration reinforces the links between town and countryside, because the spread of an urban social consciousness creates an urban bias in the rural areas, and because agriculture is increasingly dominated by an urban-based bureaucracy. As we have seen, African educational systems are almost entirely geared towards the spread of urban consciousness. Urbanization creates poverty in Africa because it takes the form of an unjust social system that imposes poverty. The institutions of this system are those that Julius Nyerere condemned, and that he called upon the Church to oppose.[6] Certainly, the Church can help the poor understand the causes of their poverty, can appeal to the conscience of the affluent, and can spearhead the 'Christian Rebellion' against poverty and injustice that Nyerere called for.[7] Christians can, for example, create their own justice and peace committees to monitor the daily harassments and abuses inflicted on them. And through social action—preferably ecumenical—they can improve the prospects of income generation, and make some attempt to correct the urban bias in education, and particularly in the mentality of rural people. Above all, the Church can help new town dwellers to capitalize their creative talents, build on the positive urban value of self-determination, and make good their right to urbanize themselves.

Urbanization and disorientation

Urban migration uproots people from their rural homeland. It creates a plural society in the town and it undermines the institutions of marriage, family and traditional community. Urban migrants are consequently both culturally and morally disoriented. Culture and morality are closely related facets of the human phenomenon because they both concern human identity and integrity. Human beings need the framework of ideas, images and behavioural norms that culture provides in order to develop, to communicate and to interact with one another. Culture gives significance to experience and is the basis for the human articulation and creation of meaning. A culturally balanced and stable community that is relatively immune to external influences can fruitfully absorb elements from other cultures, but this balance is destroyed when the community finds itself a 'cognitive minority' bombarded from all sides by alien concepts and by the irresistible contrivances of modern science and technology.[8]

This is what happens to the representatives of a given ethnic group in the modern African town. They experience a profound alienation and identity crisis. Traditional norms and the social institutions that sanctioned them are no longer at hand, while the reality principles of modern materialism are only too appealing.

Moral disorientation accompanies cultural alienation. Family life, sexual mores and the socialization of children all suffer, and crime, alcohol, drug-taking and sexual promiscuity appear as viable survival strategies. Moral disorientation also contributes to the spread of AIDS and other sexually transmitted diseases. The greater part of the despair experienced by urban-dwelling Africans stems from cultural and moral disorientation, and these ills are communicated to the countryside along the urban–rural continuum which is the high road for the dissemination of urban consciousness.

Only a genuinely multicultural Church can help Africans overcome these problems. It can do this by encouraging them to know and to develop their traditional cultures in town, and by helping them relate positively to people of other ethnic cultures. Above all, it can stimulate a process of cultural redefinition in the face of modernization, and articulate ancient cultures in new and creative ways. Inculturation is very far from being a luxury in the African urban parish. It is altogether too easy to give up the struggle for African authenticity, and to adopt Western liturgical forms and Western parish movements and structures as a solution to urban pluralism and modernity. Moral disorientation has to be tackled through community building, through support for families, through Christian formation and through parallel social action, including such things as AIDS projects.

A true *metanoia*, or conversion of heart, is the key to beneficial change in these areas. Human exploitation and alienation flourish in the town because individuals are not used to acting unilaterally or to taking responsibility for themselves and others outside the traditional structures. Within the social frameworks of parish centre, pastoral teams and basic communities, town dwellers can rebuild family relationships and forge links with people of other ethnic traditions. Even the street-gangs and other adaptive mechanisms of the slums can be put to good use in the same way. Evangelization and the inculcation of Gospel values only become effective in community experience and community action, since it is primarily in the community that the Gospel is comprehended, proclaimed and lived.

Urbanization and secularization

Evidence shows that church attendance in town and participation in urban parish life are relatively low, compared with the rural areas. It also shows that they are deteriorating in proportion to the growth of urban migration. This fact should be a major cause of concern to the Church. The Church is less visible in town than in the rural areas, and finds it harder to make headway against the materialism implied by modernization. Above all, in towns and cities, the Church does not minister to well-defined and clear-cut (ethnic) communities. As we have already seen, this indifferentism is masked by crowded urban churches and worship centres.[9] This phenomenon is doubly dangerous. It means that indifferentism is linked to a failure in ministry, and that 'crowd churches' are being created by the lack of centres.

The whole trend of Christianity today is away from the 'crowd church'. This is because it cultivates an impersonal and superficial form of commitment, and because it produces a notional and uninformed Christian faith. One reason for the success of indigenous religious movements among urban migrants is that they cultivate a close community bond among their members. A member of the Eden Revival Church in Ghana is reported to have declared: 'Edenians love their Church. They treat each other like blood relatives. There are so many Catholics, you don't even know who they are. But Edenians greet each other on the street like brothers and sisters.'[10]

During my six years in Nairobi I faced a huge congregation in St Teresa's Catholic Parish nearly every Sunday. The church could seat just over 1,000 with a bit of squeezing into the wooden benches, and on most Sundays there was nearly the same number of people standing at the back of the church and up the aisles. Even the central aisle would be half full of standing worshippers, which made the offertory and communion somewhat difficult. On weekdays, when business took me to the city centre, I was frequently hailed by people quite unknown to me. They saw me regularly at the altar and knew me well by sight. As far as I was concerned, they were part of the huge sea of faces that I looked down upon from the altar steps. The experience was symptomatic of the 'crowd church' created by urban migratory growth.

Secularism is a virus carried by modernization and urbanization. It betokens religious indifferentism, a loss of the sense of God and of the sense of sin. With the spread of urban social consciousness, towns and cities become role models for everyone, even for those living in the rural areas. We should not therefore be surprised to see a spread of secularism from the urban areas to the countryside. Moreover, since urbanization is linked to the education system, it constitutes another factor in the secularization of the educated elite.

From these facts and trends, it is clear that the Church must draw the conclusion that urban ministry is an urgent pastoral priority in Africa. No misplaced anti-urbanism should lead to a neglect of the ever-increasing urban populations. There is no doubt that dwindling rural communities must be cared for, and every effort should be made to render agriculture more profitable, but tomorrow's leaders, teachers and parents are massively present in the towns and their Christian loyalties and convictions have to be strengthened if Africa is to fulfil its promise of becoming our most Christian continent. The success of urban re-evangelization depends on increasing urban worship centres and building basic communities. It also depends on the pastoral care of youth, especially of students in higher education. Only the Church can turn the populous urban centres, from being places of dehumanization and despair, into beacons of hope and happiness, because only the Church can give the town a soul.

Urban pastoral strategies

To tackle the injustices and other evil consequences of urbanization, as well as to build on the city's positive human advantages, the Church has to operate in several social contexts and at several organizational levels. While giving primary importance to urban ministry, attention has also to be focused on the migrants' points of departure in the rural homelands. Urbanization and urban growth are less problematic in industrialized countries because there the wealth generated in the towns is more evenly distributed throughout the country. It is possible that this may happen in Africa as townships multiply in the rural areas, and long-distance migration to the primate cities is sapped by opportunities in the local townships. An important objective for Church leaders should be to create opportunities in the rural towns. This means accepting the phenomenon of urban growth and urbaniz-ation in rural parishes and co-operating constructively with it. The more that can be done to make farming pay and to invest urban wealth in the countryside, the better.

In the big urban centres, the Church has to exert maximum influence on the affluent ruling classes, the administrators, the legis-lators and the public services, so that wealth and amenities are shared and morbid factors confronted. Appealing for funds among the bour-geoisie is not sufficient. At best this becomes a form of conscience money, at worst a new form of patronage. Leaders have to be con-vinced that existing social structures are unjust and that they must be changed. The setting up of justice and peace committees at parish and diocesan levels may help to create the necessary awareness of the need for change. Co-opting the services of socially conscious investigative journalists may also help—at least in those countries where the print media enjoy a relative freedom. Probably the best hope for change will come from issue-centred groups of Christian professionals, who can exchange ideas, who can act as pressure groups, and who can give support to one another in their individual and collective professional action.

The Church's 'visibility' in the rural areas is partly the result of the relative isolation and homogeneity of its various structures. Rural parishes, sub-parishes and out-station centres are easily identifiable and more easily attract support from the surrounding settlements. In the towns and cities the structures are vastly multiplied, besides being also blurred or hidden. Co-operation should be at a premium in the town and every attempt should be made to cross its hidden frontiers. The obvious frontiers of generation, class, ethnicity and language are relativized through basic community building, and this is an indispens-able pastoral strategy in urban areas. It follows that small Christian communities have to be integrated, however loosely, with the parish associations and parish structures. An important goal of urban Christ-ian community building is to stimulate cultural education and creativity for the Church, besides the conscientization of Christians with regard to justice and peace issues.

Then, close co-operation has to be established at higher structural levels in the Church. These include the various forms of inter-parochial co-operation, those focused on the deaneries and on the level of diocesan offices and agencies. All of these bodies acquire an active pastoral relevance through their proximity to one another in the town. Co-operation among them is not simply a bonus; it is a strict necessity. Without this co-operation, their separate activities may be actually counter-productive. There also has to be co-operation between rural and urban parishes in order to follow up the cases of individual migrants and their families. This may well become a subject for study at interdiocesan level, in order to discover procedures and policies that can facilitate this ecclesial rapport between town and country.

Co-operation is also necessary, as we indicated in Chapter 10, at an ecumenical level, between the various Churches and religious denominations. Christian, and wider religious, disunity is a scandal in the relative proximity of the town. It also undermines the efficiency of social action and human development. If the town is to become a more human environment in Africa, and if urbanization is to benefit, rather than subvert, national development as a whole, then ecumenical co-operation is essential. It follows also that co-operation must be realized between Churches and both governmental and non-governmental organizations in the town. This inevitably means entering into the sphere of politics, at least at the level of local administration. Socio-economic development is a major concern of African governments and the latter readily invite co-operation from the Churches in this sphere. The Church's vindication of its right to criticize government development planning and administration constructively, and to initiate projects of its own in direct association with grass-roots communities, is not always welcome in official circles. Everything has to be done to win government confidence and to avoid being seen as a threat, a rival or a potential object of jealousy.

Finally, while on the subject of pastoral strategies, it cannot be too strongly emphasized that industrial missions have to be set up in African towns. Africa is apparently on the threshold of a massive industrialization and there is an urgent need for an evangelization of the world of industry. This will hardly be possible without the establishment of specific pastoral teams, centres and movements, and without a far-reaching measure of ecumenical and social co-operation.

Qualifications for urban Church leadership

The Nairobi Church Survey of 1986 found that only 1 per cent of the city's clergy had received any training in urban ministry.[11] This is

145

an extraordinary deficiency, when one comes to think of it. Our seminaries, Bible schools and pastoral centres offer comprehensive all-purpose courses. They do not specialize in training for urban ministry. Yet this is an urgent requirement in view of the rapidity of African urbanization and the pressing need for greater pastoral effectiveness in the towns and cities. Bishops, Church leaders and superiors of missionary societies should seriously consider making such training available. Although there are excellent courses in urban ministry offered in Europe and America, these are not necessarily well adapted to the African urban experience. What is needed is a course that takes the realities of the African urban situation into account. It may be possible to run such a course with the help of a university department of social sciences. Being urban-based, these departments have conducted a great measure of urban research over the years, although they have not usually evinced much interest in the religious aspects of the questions they have studied. The newly burgeoning third-level study-centres, created by the various Christian denominations, should seriously consider offering this kind of training.

The African urban migrant is a peasant transported to town. As our discussions of peri-urbanization and African urban culture have demonstrated, there is an urban–rural continuum. The African city cannot be understood without reference to the rural homelands from which the vast majority of its inhabitants have only recently come, and from which they are arriving daily. There is a sense in which the missionaries and pastors themselves have shared in this migratory experience. Like their charges, they have not been long in town. They, too, have come to town from the rural areas, where they have learned the tribal vernaculars and the traditional cultures. There is no doubt that this can be an asset for the urban pastor, enabling him or her to empathize more completely with the migrants, and to share in the disorienting experience of pluralism. Indeed, as we already hinted, the missionary may be more bewildered than his flock by the experience. However, as long as deeply rooted anti-urban prejudices do not persist, the pastor's rural experience may be advantageous. To have a thorough acquaintance with one ethnic culture may still be valuable in a poly-ethnic situation, as long as it does not encourage partiality. It is obviously better to be acquainted with more than one ethnic tradition, and to pick up a smattering of the major vernaculars represented in the town.

A rural experience is valuable because it is an introduction to a whole pattern of thinking and a whole way of life, which still remains the focus of interest for the average urban migrant, and which still remains the yardstick against which urban events are judged and understood. Urban culture in Africa is, we have said, a reinterpretation of interacting rural cultures confronted by modernization. Therefore, to understand the urban situation, it helps to have been rurally inculturated.

However, in making this point, there is no wish to play down the special nature of urbanization itself, or to suggest that an initiation to urban ministry is not also necessary. The missionary with rural experience quickly finds that rural methods and routines do not work in the urban situation. Whatever their antecedents and their long-term preoccupations, African townspeople do not wish to be treated like country folk; nor do they deserve to be. The urban pastor must therefore come to the African town with an open mind and, still more to the point, with open eyes and ears.

For this reason, one need not exclude the possibility of a pastor or missionary coming to town without the previous experience of a rural ministry. He or she would hopefully come with no anti-urban prejudice, and with a wholehearted commitment to the Church in the town with all its peculiarities and special characteristics. On the other hand, it would be eminently desirable for such a person to cultivate an acquaintance with some of the rural homelands to which urban Christians so frequently return. An acquaintance with the rural areas is also necessary if one is to appreciate the full impact of urbanization in Africa, its causes and its consequences. Needless to say, the urban pastor also needs the highest professional and vocational qualifications in order to deal with people of every class and educational background, and in order to understand the socio-economic mechanisms of the city. Considerable strength of character is needed, too, for coping with the so-called morbid factors of the slums and squatter areas.

A final word

George Orwell predicted an endless future conflict between East and West, with a marginal Third World—including, perhaps, Africa—as the battleground. The year 1984, however, has come and gone, and we are now witnessing the decline of superpower confrontation in the world. Yet it still looks as if Africa will remain the marginal continent for the foreseeable future, the world's dumping ground, laid waste by international debt, transnational exploitation and the nefarious effect of the arms trade. 'When elephants fight', says the Swahili proverb, 'it is the grass that suffers.' Africa's hope of a better, alternative future rests on controlling the modernization process and on cultivating her own appropriate technologies. Urbanization is two-faced. It can remain a vehicle of exploitation and alienation, or it can become the necessary vehicle for valid development.

There is, however, no way in which the tide of urbanization can be turned back. It will continue to flood through the continent until, at the end of the first quarter of the coming century, half Africa's population will be town or city dwelling. The Christian task in Africa is the evangelization of a continent in the process of rapid urbanization. In fact, it is, to a great extent, the evangelization of the urbanization process itself. If the Gospel of Christ makes a lasting impact in Africa, it will be because it has helped the urban process to become less invidious and less unjust, more human and more enduringly creative. It will have given the African town a soul.

References

1 Soyinka 1973, pp. 79–112.

2 Cf. Harrison 1987, *passim*.

3 Ibid., p. 63.

4 McDonagh 1986, p. 128.

5 Nyerere 1973, pp. 215–27.

6 Ibid.

7 Ibid.

8 Berger 1980, pp. 32–65.

9 Cf. Chapter 5 above.

10 Beckman 1975, p. 86.

11 Downes *et al.* 1989, p. 45.

Bibliography

Anderson, N., 1955, *The Metropolis in Modern Life*, New York, 4 vols.

Anderson, N., 1960, *The Urban Community*, New York.

Anderson, N., 1964, *Urbanism and Urbanization*, Leiden.

Banton, M., 1957, *West African City: A Study of Tribal Life in Freetown*, London.

Beckman, D. M., 1975, *Eden Revival: Spiritual Churches in Ghana*, St Louis, MO.

Berger, P. L., 1980, *The Heretical Imperative*, London.

Blixen, K., 1937, *Out of Africa*, London (1980).

Boff, L., 1986, *Ecclesiogenesis: The Base Communities Reinvent the Church*, London.

Broos, L., 1988, *Maadili ya Uganga*, Tabora, 3 vols.

Bunting, I. D., 1989, *Claiming the Urban Village*, Grove Books, Nottingham.

Burgman, H., 1982, 'New Urban Apostolate in Kisumu', *African Ecclesial Review*, vol. 24, no. 6, pp. 337–42.

Burgman, H., 1983, 'Urban Apostolate in Kisumu (2)', *African Ecclesial Review*, vol. 25, no. 1, pp. 7–15.

CAFOD (Catholic Fund for Overseas Development) 1990, *AIDS and Development*, London.

Clark, D., 1984, *The Liberation of the Church*, Birmingham.

Clarke, P. A. B., 1988, *AIDS: Medicine, Politics and Society*, London.

Clyde-Mitchell, J., 1969, *Social Networks in Urban Situations*, Oxford.

Cohen, A., 1969, *Custom and Politics in Urban Africa*, London.

Comblin, J., 1968, *La Théologie de la Ville*, Paris.

Cosstick, V. (ed.), 1987, *AIDS: Meeting the Community Challenge*, Slough.

Dallape, F., 1987, *An Experience with Street Children*, Nairobi.

Davis, M., 1967, *Modern Industry and the African*, London.

de Jong, D., 1979, 'Community Building in Urban Area', *African Ecclesial Review*, vol. 20, no. 4, pp. 307–9.

Denis, Brother, 1990, *Kanisa*, Taizé.

Dewey, A. G., 1970, 'Ritual as a Mechanism for Urban Adaptation', *Man*, vol. 5, no. 3, pp. 438–48.

Downes, S., *et al.*, 1989, *Summary of the Nairobi Church Survey*, Nairobi.

Edele, A., 1977, 'Building Community—Case Study from Lusaka', *African Ecclesial Review*, vol. 19, no. 2, pp. 90–100.

Elkan, W., 1960, *Migrants and Proletarians*, London.

Fichter, J., 1960, 'Can the Urban Parish be a Community?', *Gregorianum*, vol. 41, pp. 393–423.

Fliche, A. and Martin, V. (eds), 1959, *Histoire de l'Eglise*, vol. 12a (Le Bras, G.), Paris.

Fontaine, J. S., 1970, 'Two Types of Youth Groups in Kinshasa' in Banton, M. (ed.), *Socialization: The Approach from Social Anthropology*, London, pp. 191–213.

Frankenberg, R., 1966, *Communities in Britain*, Harmondsworth.

Gilbert, A. and Gugler, J., 1981 (1989), *Cities, Poverty and Development: Urbanization in the Third World*, Oxford.

Grol, A., 1982, 'Undugu and the Parking Boys', *Spiritus*, no. 23/86, pp. 3–16.

Gulick, J., 1989, *The Humanity of Cities*, Granby, MA.

Hake, A., 1971, 'An Urban Industrial Ministry in Kenya' in Barrett, D. B. (ed.), *African Initiatives in Religion*, Nairobi, pp. 242–52.

Hake, A., 1977, *African Metropolis: Nairobi's Self-Help City*, London.

Hanna, W. J. and J. L., 1971, *Urban Dynamics in Black Africa*, New York.

Harrison, P., 1987, *The Greening of Africa*, London.

Harvey, A., 1989, *Theology in the City*, London.

Houtart, F., 1955, 'Faut-il abandonner la paroisse dans la ville moderne?', *Nouvelle Revue Théologique*, vol. 87, pp. 602–13.

Houtart, F., 1961, 'Vers une pastorale urbaine', *Social Compass*, vol. 8/6, pp. 559–65.

Houtart, F., 1963, 'Sociologie de la paroisse comme assemblée eucharistique' in Houtart, F., *Paroisse et Liturgie*, Louvain, p. 564.

Joinet, B., 1985, 'Networks or the Economy of Solidarity', *Letter to my Superiors*, no. 4, Dar es Salaam.

Kalilombe, P. A., 1984, *From Outstations to Small Christian Communities*, Gaba Spearhead no. 82/83.

Kaunda, K. and Morris, C., 1966, *A Humanist in Africa*, London.

Kavanaugh, J. F., 1985, 'Capitalist Culture and the Christian Faith', *The Way*, vol. 25, no. 3, pp. 175–85.

Kelley, J., 1977, *The Church in the Town*, Gaba Spearhead no. 47.

Kubai, M., 1985, 'Wakulima Porters Are Now Men!' *The Standard*, Nairobi, Saturday 25 May, p. 8.

Kuper, H., 1965, *Urbanization and Migration in West Africa*, London.

Little, K., 1974, *Urbanization as a Social Process*, London.

McDonagh, S., 1986, *To Care for the Earth*, London/Santa Fe, NM.

Mann, J., 1989, 'Global AIDS into the 1990s', *World Health* (WHO), October, pp. 6–7.

Martin, C. and P., 1978, *Cargoes of the East*, London.

Mathew, D., 1960, 'The Training of an African Clergy', *The Month*, October, vol. 24, no. 4, p. 201.

Mayer, P., 1970, 'Socialization by Peers—The Youth Organization of the Red Xhosa' in Banton, M. (ed.), *Socialization: The Approach from Social Anthropology*, London, pp. 159–89.

Mayer, P. and I., 1961, *Townsmen or Tribesmen?*, Oxford.

Meadows, M., 1969, *Urbanism, Urbanization and Change*, London.

Metz, J. B., 1980, *Faith in History and Society*, London.

Miner, H., 1967, *The City in Modern Africa*, London.

Mumford, L., 1961, *The Culture of Cities*, New York.

Nunn, P., 1987, 'AIDS and the Developing World' in Cosstick, V. (ed.), *AIDS: The Community Challenge*, Slough, pp. 25–31.

Nyerere, J. K., 1973, *Freedom and Development*, Oxford.

Obudho, R. A. and Mhlanga, C. C., 1988, *Slum and Squatter Settlements in Sub-Saharan Africa*, New York.

O'Connor, A., 1983 (1986), *The African City*, London.

Oram, N., 1965, *Towns in Africa*, London.

Padian, N. S., 1988, 'Prostitute Women and AIDS: Epidemiology', *AIDS*, vol. 2, no. 6, pp. 421–28.

Parkin, D., 1969, *Neighbours and Nationals in an African City Ward*, London.

Parkin, D., 1975, *Town and Country in Central and Eastern Africa*, London.

Paul VI, Pope, 1975, *Evangelization in the Modern World (Evangelii Nuntiandi)*, London.

Peil, M. (ed.), 1982, *African Cities and Communities*, Gaba Spearhead no. 72.

Perrin-Jassy, M.-F., 1973, *Basic Communities in the African Churches*, New York.

Ranger, T. O. and Weller, J. (eds), 1975, *Themes in the Christian History of Central Africa*, London.

Rigby, P. and Lule, F., 1971, 'Divination and Healing in Peri-Urban Kampala', Social Science Conference Paper, Makerere University.

Roberts, B., 1978, *Cities of Peasants*, London.

Shorter, A., 1973, *African Culture and the Christian Church*, London.

Shorter, A., 1974, *East African Societies*, London.

Shorter, A., 1978, *African Christian Spirituality*, London.

Shorter, A., 1983a, *White Fathers—Urban Pastoral Project*, Tabora.

Shorter, A., 1983b, 'Town and Country Apostolate in East Africa', *African Ecclesial Review*, vol. 25, no. 6, pp. 362–68.

Shorter, A., 1988, *Toward a Theology of Inculturation*, London.

Southall, A. W., 1961, *Social Change in Modern Africa*, London.

Southall, A. W. and Gutkind, P. J., 1957, *Townsmen in the Making*, Kampala.

Soyinka, W., 1973, *Collected Plays*, vol. 1, Oxford.

Stanley, H. M., 1899, *Through the Dark Continent*, London, 2 vols.

Swantz, M. L., 1970, *Ritual and Symbol*, Uppsala.

Tessier, R. (ed.), 1983, *Young People in African Towns*, Gaba Spearhead no. 79.

Tessier, R. (ed.), 1984, *Pastoral Care of Youth in Rural Africa*, Gaba Spearhead no. 81.

Thomas, N., 1975, 'Inter-Church Co-operation in Rhodesia's Towns 1962–1972' in Ranger, T. O. and Weller, J. (eds), *Themes in the Christian History of Central Africa*, London, pp. 238–55.

Turner, V. W., 1969, *The Ritual Process*, London.

Van Huet, E., 1968, *Urban Apostolate in Dar es Salaam*, Gaba Pastoral Paper, no. 6.

Zanotelli, A., 1988, 'Facing the Problems of Rapid Urbanization', *African Ecclesial Review*, vol. 30, no. 5, pp. 277–84.

Biblical quotations are taken from the Bible Society's *Chain Reference Bible*, Collins, London, 1976. References to Canon Law are from the Canon Law Society of Great Britain and Ireland, *The Code of Canon Law*, London, 1983. References to the Second Vatican Council documents are to Flannery, A., *Vatican Council II*, Dublin, 1975.